# 100 Literacy Hours

## YEAR R

Published by Scholastic Ltd,
Villiers House,
Clarendon Avenue,
Leamington Spa,
Warwickshire CV32 5PR

Text © 1999 Wendy Jolliffe, Kathleen Taylor
and David Waugh

3 4 5 6 7 8 9  9 0 1 2 3 4 5 6 7

SERIES CONCEPT
**Chris Webster**

AUTHORS
**Wendy Jolliffe
Kathleen Taylor
David Waugh**

EDITOR
**Irene Goodacre**

ASSISTANT EDITORS
**Christine Lee
Roanne Davis**

SERIES DESIGNER
**Joy White**

DESIGNER
**Mark Udall**

COVER ARTWORK
**Peter Stevenson**

ILLUSTRATIONS
**Sami Sweeten**

British Library Cataloguing-in-Publication Data
A catalogue record for this book is available from the British Library.

ISBN 0-590-53924-8

ACKNOWLEDGEMENTS

The publishers gratefully acknowledge permission to reproduce the following copyright material:

**Candlewick Press Inc, Cambridge, MA.,** for the use of text and an adapted illustration from *Little Lumpty* by Miko Imai © 1994, Miko Imai (1994, Candlewick Press, Cambridge, Massachusetts, USA).
**Faber & Faber** for the use of 'Telling' by Wendy Cope from *Twiddling Your Thumbs* by Wendy Cope © 1988, Wendy Cope (1988, Faber & Faber).
**Julia Matthews** for the use of 'Number One, touch your tongue' by Julia Matthews from *Bright Ideas Teacher Handbooks: Language Resources* © 1987, Julia Matthews (1987, Scholastic Ltd).
**Pamela Mordecai** for the use of 'Caribbean Counting Rhyme' from *Twinkle, Twinkle Chocolate Bar* compiled by John Foster © 1991, Pamela Mordecai (1991, OUP).
**Rony Robinson** for the use of 'We've got a Wa Wa' from *A Very First Poetry Book* compiled by John Foster © 1984, Rony Robinson (1984, OUP).

# Contents

**INTRODUCTION**  Page 4

**TERM 1**  Page 21

Naming Names  22
Nursery Rhymes  24
Little Lumpty  34
Introducing Non-fiction  38
Alphabet Books  47
The Gingerbread Man (1)  55
The Gingerbread Man (2)  63
Reading Notices and Signs  69
Writing Notices and Signs  71

**TERM 2**  Page 75

Dear Zoo  76
Dear Farm  85
Animals  91
Pets  96
Counting Rhymes  100
Twinkle Twinkle Chocolate Bar  109
All Kinds of Food  116
Don't Forget the Bacon!  122

**TERM 3**  Page 127

Each Peach Pear Plum  128
Hunt the Word  134
My Day  136
Our Class  142
Goldilocks and The Three Bears (1)  151
Goldilocks and The Three Bears (2)  157
Action Rhymes  162
Toys (1)  167
Toys (2)  171
The Slug  174

# INTRODUCTION

## ABOUT THE SERIES

*100 Literacy Hours* is a series of year-specific teachers' resource books that provides a core of material for the teaching of the English curriculum within the context of the *National Literacy Strategy Framework for Teaching* and within the structure of the Literacy Hour. Each book offers term-by-term lesson plans, complete with objectives and organization grids and accompanied, where relevant, by photocopiable texts and activity sheets. The materials are ready-to-use, and their adaptable format enables them to be used as flexibly as possible. The 100 hours provided offer a balance of both reading and writing, and of range: fiction and poetry and non-fiction. However, it is expected that you will wish to personalize the material – altering the order, interleaving lesson plans with complementary materials from your school's existing schemes, consolidating work by using the structure of a lesson plan as a model for a lesson with different content, and so on. The loose-leaf format of each book, with hole-punched, perforated, tear-out pages, makes the integration of other tried-and-tested and favourite material into the core very easy.

## USING THIS BOOK

### The materials

This book provides 100 literacy hours for Reception, presented as 'units' of between 1 and 5 hours. There is a balance of reading and writing units, most of which are linked in order to demonstrate and reinforce the close relationship. The units are fully supported with detailed lesson plans and integrated photocopiable resources. Together, these materials should be regarded as a core, and a starting point for developing your own personalized folder for the year.

### Adapting and personalizing the materials

During the trialling of these resources, wide differences in ability were found in classes of the same year group in different schools. This means that the precise content of the plans and resources will almost certainly need modification to suit the children in a particular school. One way to do this is as follows:
■ Separate the pages of the book and place them in an A4 ringbinder.
■ Adjust the level of the photocopiable resource sheets to match the needs of the pupils in your year group.
■ 'Trade' materials with higher or lower year groups so that the average level matches that of the target year group.
■ Add your own favourite teaching materials in the appropriate places.
■ Substitute materials for others if necessary (for example, if you have a set of books which you wish to use instead of one of the ones recommended).
You will then have created a tailor-made folder of plans and resources for your year group.

### Preparing a scheme of work

All schools are required to write detailed schemes of work, and these materials have been designed to facilitate this process. The termly Overview Grids on pages 14–19 have been compiled by extracting the 'Objectives' grids from each teaching unit to provide you with what are, essentially, medium-term plans. These grids are photocopiable so, should you wish to alter the order of units and/or add your own, they can be copied, cut and pasted to make your own plans.

## ORGANIZATION OF TEACHING UNITS

Each term is divided into teaching units comprising between 1–5 hours. Each of the main units has either a reading or a writing focus (although there is, of course, overlap) and a fiction, poetry or non-fiction content. The units are organized as follows:

## OBJECTIVES GRID

Outlines the word-, sentence- and text-level objectives of the unit.

| UNIT | SPELLING/VOCABULARY | GRAMMAR/PUNCTUATION | COMPREHENSION/ COMPOSITION |
|------|---------------------|---------------------|----------------------------|
| WRITING NON-FICTION Simple non-fiction texts: A toy alphabet. | Identify and write initial and dominant phonemes in spoken words. | Expect written text to make sense and check for sense if it does not. | Begin to make notes from non-fiction books by drawing pictures. |

## ORGANIZATION GRID

Outlines the key activities for each part of each hour.

| | INTRODUCTION | WHOLE-CLASS SKILLS WORK | DIFFERENTIATED GROUP ACTIVITIES | CONCLUSION |
|---|--------------|------------------------|--------------------------------|------------|
| HOUR 1 | Read an enlarged book on toys with simple text. Model early note-making by drawing pictures to match the text. | Using a selection of toys in a bag, choose a toy and ask the children to help you write the word, talking about the different sounds and how they are written. | 1*: Guided writing of early note-making. 2: Make a toy alphabet, using a selection of pictures. 3: Match pictures of toys to the correct initial letter. | Show examples of note-making, with different children describing what their pictures show. Work with the whole class to think of examples of different toys to match a few letters of the alphabet. Write the words with pupils suggesting how they are spelled. |
| HOUR 2 | Show the children the pictures modelled in the previous hour and write sentences to match at their suggestion. | Continue with the toy alphabet using real toys or pictures and writing the words at the pupils' suggestion. Talk about choosing letters for each phoneme. | 1: Make a toy alphabet, using a selection of pictures and writing appropriate words. 2*: Guided writing of early note-making. 3: Sort pictures of toys into groups beginning with the same letter. | Show some examples of note-making and toy alphabets. Reinforce how letters are written in response to different phonemes by choosing various toys and writing the words. |

## UNIT LESSON PLANS

Each unit of lesson plans is written to the following headings:

### Resources
Provides a list of what you need for teaching the whole unit. Where appropriate, in the longer units, these have been grouped into paragraphs for ease of reference, for example: common classroom resources, photocopiable pages, other items.

### Preparation
Outlines any advance preparation needed before the hour(s) begins. Where appropriate, in longer units, these have been grouped by hour.

Each hour is then set out as follows:

### Introduction
Describes the activities for the whole-class shared reading/writing session.

### Whole-class skills work
Describes the activities for the whole-class word- and sentence-level skills session. (See page 8 for further information about whole-class skills work.)
   **[NB: Sometimes Introduction and Whole-class skills work have been combined under one heading.]**

### Differentiated group work
Describes the group activities for the guided or shared group and independent work session. (See page 9 for further information about differentiated group work.)

### Conclusion
Sets out what to do in the whole-class plenary session.

### Photocopiables
Photocopiable texts and activity sheets are provided to support each unit. These can be found at the end of each relevant unit and are marked with the photocopiable symbol. Some sheets have more than one application and are referred to in several units.

## READING UNITS

These teaching units have three aims:
■ to develop reading skills across a wide range of texts – fiction, poetry and non-fiction
■ to develop skills of comprehension at a literal and inferential level
■ to encourage enjoyment of reading.

### Using the texts
Some texts are provided on photocopiable resource sheets. In addition, the following popular texts will also be needed:

• *Little Lumpty* by Miko Imai, Walker, ISBN 0-7445-3605-7
• *Dear Zoo* by Rod Campbell, Picture Puffin, ISBN 0-14-050446-X
• *Twinkle Twinkle Chocolate Bar* compiled by John Foster, OUP ISBN 0-19-276125-0
• *Don't Forget the Bacon!* by P. Hutchins, Picture Puffin, ISBN 0-14-050315-3
• *Each Peach Pear Plum* by Janet and Allan Ahlberg, Picture Puffin, ISBN 0-14-050919-4
• *All About You* by Catherine and Laurence Anholt, Mammoth, ISBN 0-7497-1297-X
• *Toys* by Bobbie Neate, Longman Book Project Starter Book, ISBN 0-582 12277 5
• Any Big Book of nursery rhymes, containing Little Miss Muffet, Hickory Dickory Dock, Jack and Jill, Hey Diddle Diddle and Humpty Dumpty
• Examples of fiction and non-fiction Big Books
• A set of a patterned and rhyming text
• A set of non-fiction recount books
• Any animal alphabet book
• Any animal non-fiction text including a Big Book version
• A selection of poetry books
• A selection of non-fiction books on toys

The following texts are also recommended:

• *My Day* by Barrie Wade, Pathways, Collins Educational, ISBN 0-00-30150-3
• *What's the Time, Mr Wolf?* by Colin Hawkins, Mammoth, ISBN 0-7497-1747-5
• *Okki-Tokki-Unga Action Songs,* A & C Black, ISBN 0-7136-4078-2
• Examples of thematic alphabet books such as *Alfie's Alphabet* by Shirley Hughes, Red Fox, ISBN 0-09-922042-3
• Examples of flap books, such as *Noisy Farm* by Rod Campbell, Picture Puffin, ISBN 0-14-050293 9
• Big Book versions of *Each Peach Pear Plum* by Janet and Allan Ahlberg, Oliver and
• Boyd, ISBN 0-05-004406-0; *Goldilocks and the Three Bears* (eg Kingscourt, Literacy
• Links, Catalogue no. 60425) and *The Gingerbread Man*
• Wordless version of *Goldilocks and the Three Bears*
• Small version of *Goldilocks and the Three Bears*

Full details of these texts appear in the resources section of each unit. All the texts are intended for use as shared texts, ie texts for whole-class and/or guided reading. Use of appropriate teaching methods enables children to read and understand texts beyond their independent reading level. The methods suggested in these materials include:
■ preparation: eg giving the background to a story, prior study of difficult words
■ shared reading to the whole class with children following the text
■ differentiated follow-up activities which allow the most able children to respond independently to the text while further support is given to weaker readers
■ guided reading, in which the teacher takes groups of children through the text helping them with phonic or contextual clues (less able readers), or higher-level reading skills (more able readers).

Additional suggestions are given, where relevant, in the detailed lesson plans – for example, use of different versions of the same story. It is assumed that children will be following a programme of guided reading alongside their reading of these shared texts.

### Written comprehension

Most written tasks included in these materials encourage a creative response to reading. These often reveal children's comprehension of the text as clearly as any formal comprehension, and, like the oral and dramatic activities, they are just as effective in developing comprehension skills. Activities included in the units will support the development of these skills.

# WRITING UNITS

The writing units provide a series of structured writing experiences throughout the year. Some writing will be done with the teacher or another adult, and some will be done with the teacher modelling writing, but using the children's suggestions. These shared writing sessions should enable the teacher to use the vocabulary of writing and to discuss approaches to presentation. The teacher should also be able to demonstrate that writing can be revised and redrafted to make it more accessible to an audience.

There are also many opportunities for children to write independently, but at Key Stage 1 it is particularly important to provide props such as word banks (see Additional Resources, page 10) and frameworks which children can draw upon. These props should enable the children to become more independent to allow the teacher more time to work with children during differentiated group sessions.

### Cross-curricular writing

Many opportunities for non-narrative writing occur in other curriculum areas. Therefore, when the necessary skills have been introduced through one of the non-fiction units, they should be applied to another curriculum area soon afterwards.

# SPEAKING AND LISTENING

Speaking and Listening is also an essential part of literacy, and development of skills in this important area has been integrated into the units for both reading and writing. Speaking and listening is the most important way of developing reading skills. Children need to explore texts through discussion, role play and other forms of oral 'comprehension' before they can write with greater understanding. Brainstorming, sharing ideas, helping each other to check work and so on, will all help children to write more effectively.

# TIMING OF THE LITERACY HOUR

A brisk pace is an important feature of an effective literacy hour. The following suggestions will help to keep things moving:

■ Train children to work independently. Stress that you cannot help them while you are working with a group – their turn will come. In the meantime, they must find out for themselves, or ask a friend or a classroom assistant.
■ Keep explanations brief. Get children on task as soon as possible, and give further clarification and help in the context of the activity. The use of a Task Management Board may help by acting as a visual reminder of group tasks. This uses symbols to denote activities (which can be created by the class) and 'T' to denote when working with the teacher. Groups are listed or named down the left-hand side of the board and the symbols put along side each group. If the symbols are laminated and backed with Velcro or Blu-Tack, they can be easily moved around and re-used.
■ Don't let skills sessions over-run, unless there is a good reason which has been planned for previously. Skills will be revised and practised several times throughout the year within the context of other slots in the Literacy Hour and in other lessons in English and other curricular areas.
■ When starting group activities sessions, give a clear message about what you want children to have achieved in the time allocated, and encourage them to work efficiently – ask them to concentrate on written tasks and complete illustrations later.

■ When working with a group, sit in a position so that the rest of the class can be seen.
■ Break off group work immediately to deal with any disruption. Ensure that children are aware that they are being supervised even when you are working with a group.

### Introductory session: Shared reading

The following procedure is recommended:

■ Select a specific focus in advance (for example, rhyming words).
■ Begin by predicting the contents of the text from the cover and title (and blurb if appropriate).
■ Discuss words in the title, look at the title page and other illustrations. (This is an important step in activating children's prior knowledge, which is vital in a meaningful learning context.)
■ Read the text at a brisk expressive pace with the children joining in and use a pointer to point to the words as you read. This will help to emphasize the one-to-one correspondence of one spoken word to one written word, and focus the children to the text. Ensure that you use a pointer, as fingers will mask the text.
■ During reading, stop occasionally (but not so frequently that the meaning is lost) to ask questions or predict what will happen next.
■ Demonstrate using different cues, for example, picture cues or graphophonic cues, ie 'How can we work out this tricky word?' You can also demonstrate reading on and leaving a word out, but guessing it later, or reading back to find out a difficult word, depending on the position of the word in the sentence.
■ After reading, respond to the text by asking questions to ensure understanding of the content. Extend by asking questions which require an inferential understanding.
■ Focus on specific sentence or word-level aspects after ensuring an understanding of the whole text.
■ Use a variety of guided and independent tasks to deepen understanding, and to explore word- and sentence-level aspects. The units contain a large number of tasks of this nature.

### Whole-class skills work

It is during these sessions that grammar, punctuation, spelling, vocabulary and phonic skills are taught, with an emphasis on word-level work at Key Stage One. The main principle is that the skills arise from the shared text and will also be used in the related writing unit. Over the year, key skills should be revisited many times so that the children's mastery of them grows incrementally.

Although the materials in this book include spelling activities based on spelling rules and patterns arising from the texts, they cannot take the place of a programme of individualized spelling for children. The children could collect, in a spelling book, a list of words they need to learn. This could be supplemented at least once a week with words from a standard list to make a list of, say, ten (or more for more able/older children). Children then learn their lists using the 'Look, say, cover, write, check' strategy. Pairs of children can test each other on their own lists. Any words not learned can be carried over into the next list.

At Key Stage One there should be considerable emphasis on the following:

■ listening to the sounds within words and identifying phonemes
■ identifying initial sounds
■ simple mnemonics to help children to remember spellings
■ spelling patterns
■ segmenting words into onset and rime and into graphemes which represent phonemes.

*A NOTE ON TEACHING PHONICS*
There are three main strands in the teaching of phonics:

*Phonological awareness*
Children must be able to hear and discriminate sounds in words accurately. It is important to assess children's ability to do this and provide plenty of opportunities to develop the use of rhythm, rhyme and alliteration for those who have not yet developed good phonological awareness.

*Sound/symbol (Phoneme/grapheme) correspondence*
One teaching programme which helps develop this correspondence is THRASS. This stands for Teaching Handwriting Reading and Spelling Skills. Central to THRASS is the chart which shows how all 44 sounds (phonemes) of spoken English are represented by letters (graphemes). THRASS focuses on knowledge of the alphabet and the naming of the lower-case letters and their capitals, using the correct terms from the beginning (eg phoneme and grapheme). THRASS also teaches that it is not always one letter which makes one sound (a graph); it may be two letters (a digraph) or three letters (a trigraph).

Mnemonics: Many phonic schemes (for example, *Letterland*, or *The Phonic Handbook: Jolly Phonics*) utilize mnemonics to help children to remember the sound/symbol relationship. These are useful as an interim measure in helping children to recall the letter and the sound(s) it makes.

*Blending/segmenting sounds*
Children need to be taught to blend individual phonemes into words when reading and to segment words into sounds for spelling in order to use phonics successfully.

## Differentiated group activities

For most group activities, three levels of differentiation are suggested:

Group 1:  above average pupils
Group 2:  average pupils
Group 3:  below average pupils.

The ability groups may be further subdivided according to size of class and ability of the children. Groups do not have to be of equal size and there may be some flexibility of groupings.

In the average Key Stage One class, group sizes would be between 8–10 (with some trade-off between groups according to the spread of ability in the class). This is fine for organizational purposes and working with the teacher, but too large for most collaborative activities. These groups will therefore need to be subdivided into smaller groups of fours or pairs for some activities.

Try to divide your teaching time equally between all groups over the course of the week – the most able need help just as much as the least able if they are given suitably demanding tasks.

**[NB: An asterisk (\*) after the group number is used on the grids and in the lesson plans to show which groups the teacher should be working with during the group activities session.]**

Finally, it is important to stress that even when you are working intensively with one group, the first priority is always the overall work rate of the whole class. See 'Timing of the Literacy Hour' (page 7) for suggestions on how to keep the session moving at a brisk pace.

## Finishing off

At the end of the group activities, it may be that some children have not completed their work. If this is the case, children could complete short tasks as homework. Some tasks may be completed over several sessions, for example if they are making their own books. However, it is important to stress to children what they are expected to finish within the time and thereby ensure the pace of work.

## Conclusion

The key objective in most of these sessions is to review the teaching points of the lesson and ensure that the work of selected children, pairs or groups is shared with the class for discussion and evaluation. Enough should be heard to exemplify the variety of work produced, but not so much that it becomes boring, or takes too much time. Keep a record of who has presented what to ensure that all children have the opportunity to present their work in due course.

**[NB: On entry to school, children in Reception classes are not required by the National Literacy Strategy to be working a full literacy hour. It is intended that Reception and early years classes will incorporate elements of the literacy hour gradually, introducing the full hour during the third term of the Reception year.]**

## ASSESSMENT

Regular and on-going assessment of pupils' achievements and progress is, of course, essential. These materials assume that you and your school have satisfactory methods and systems of assessing and recording already in place and therefore don't attempt to suggest an alternative. However, what these materials also assume is that your current procedures are based on clearly stated teaching objectives. Therefore the objectives grids at the beginning of each unit should be invaluable in providing you with a framework for on-going assessment.

In addition, to facilitate individual pupil conferencing at the end of each half-term, a photocopiable record sheet has been provided on page 20. Specific targets for reading and writing can be set for each pupil at the end of the previous half-term and recorded on the sheet in the left-hand column. Interim progress towards these targets can be assessed when appropriate and noted in the middle column. Then, at the end of each half-term, during the conference, pupil and teacher together can record achievement and agree further targets for the next half-term.

## ADDITIONAL RESOURCES

The following additional equipment and resources are invaluable in delivering the Literacy Hour, and are referred to in a number of units:
■ Big Book stand
■ Whiteboard/magnetic board and letters
■ Pointer (a home-made one will do!)
■ OHP and acetate sheets
■ 'Post-it' notes
■ Masking cards – which slide to reveal particular words (see below for details)
■ Selection of ready-made blank cards for writing key vocabulary
■ Listening centre and headphones
■ Blank Big Books
■ Bank of frequently used resources for independent group work, such as word wheels, word dice, rhyming pictures, letter dice, words squares, sight word recognition games, for example lotto and pairs. A range of these resources is provided in these materials for specific activities
■ Resource box for each table, containing, for example, spelling resources (spelling cards, dictionaries, personal dictionaries, 'have a go' books), pencils, crayons, sharpeners, rubbers, scissors, glue, highlighters.

### Big Books

Big Books are an essential resource for many of the literacy hour lessons. When purchasing commercially-made versions (some are specifically recommended in the units), ensure that the print is large enough to be seen by the whole class and look for examples which will provide a rich resource for different activities.

*Making Big Books from published books*
It is possible to make your own Big Books using published picture books. You will need to cut the book up into pages (if the book has pictures on both sides of the pages, you will need two copies). Then retype the text using 48-point font size and double spacing in between the words. Stick the pictures onto A3 size card or stiff paper and stick the appropriate enlarged words underneath. Laminate the pages and include the cover, title page and so on, so the whole book is reproduced. Now bind the book, using either a spiral binder, or several binding rings. Note that only one Big Book (not multiple copies) may be made for any one published picture book.

*Making a blank Big Book*
You will need sheets of standard-sized large card (64cm by 45cm), sheets of buff sugar paper cut to fit the card so that a 3cm margin remains all the way round, and some sticky-backed plastic cut into strips measuring 8cm wide and slightly longer than the length of the pages.
   Use one side only of the buff sugar paper pages when scribing the story for the children (write in large print), and decide together on the amount of illustration space.

Once the illustrations have been completed, mount each sugar paper page onto a sheet of card in the correct order, using both sides of the card, to make the pages of the book. Take a strip of sticky-backed plastic and carefully lay the edge of the cover page about 3cm into the strip leaving a little at the top and bottom (Figure 1a). Place the edge of the second page alongside the edge of the first page and make a seam with a second length of sticky-backed plastic (Figure 1b). Do this until all the pages are linked together with the sticky-backed plastic seams. Finish by sticking the remaining width of sticky-backed plastic to the back cover.

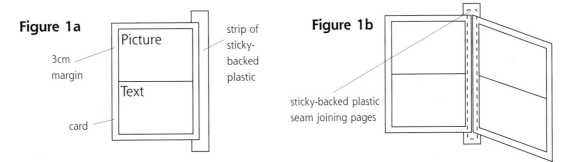

**Figure 1a**

3cm margin — Picture / Text — card — strip of sticky-backed plastic

**Figure 1b**

sticky-backed plastic seam joining pages

### Enlarged texts

A large variety of enlarged texts can be used for shared reading. For example, commercially produced posters, nursery rhyme cards and poems are available from publishers. Home-made posters and shaped poem cards can also be made by typing the text (again in 48-point font size) and adding illustrations from photocopiable sheets or children's own illustrations. Shaped poem cards are made by using an enlarged shape, for example of a pig, and then fixing on a suitable poem or rhyme. Laminate or cover in sticky-backed plastic for extended use. With the text extracts provided in this book you can make enlarged A3 versions using the photocopier.

### Storyboards

An enlarged storyboard on which you can fix characters and objects from a story is useful to focus young children on the story and help fix the details in their minds. To make one, use a large sheet of chipboard or hardboard measuring about 75cm high by 90cm wide and cover in felt. Now cut appropriate characters to fit the story out of different coloured felt, or use cardboard and attach a patch of Velcro to the back (you can build up a selection of characters for traditional tales). The characters will stick to the felt board. Alternatively, if you have a magnetic board, cut the characters or objects out of stiff cardboard and colour or paint them, then fix magnetic tape to the back of them.

### Word banks

Word banks can take many forms. You can provide lists of words which children will need for general use (for example, the high frequency lists in the *National Literacy Strategy Framework for Teaching*) and/or lists of words for specific activities or topics.

The words may be provided on sheets of paper or they may be displayed so that children can refer to them constantly and use them as part of their 'Look, say, cover, write, check' strategy.

You could make a pocket wall display. This will consist of a large piece of cloth (such as very strong cotton) approximately 1.5m wide and 1m long, onto which are stitched pockets large enough to house high frequency words printed onto card. The letters of the alphabet in lower and upper case will need to be displayed on the outside of the pockets. (You could combine x y z on one pocket.) Alternatively this could

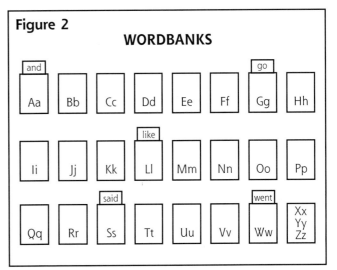

**Figure 2**

**WORDBANKS**

and · Aa · Bb · Cc · Dd · Ee · Ff · go · Gg · Hh

Ii · Jj · Kk · like · Ll · Mm · Nn · Oo · Pp

said · Qq · Rr · Ss · Tt · Uu · Vv · went · Ww · Xx Yy Zz

be made from strong card with cardboard pockets. (See Figure 2.)

When new words are added, use the opportunity to discuss spelling and alphabetical order and ask the children to help you place the new words in the correct positions. Encourage the children to go to the word bank to see if spellings they need are displayed rather than asking for your help. Discuss the words regularly and make sure that children become increasingly familiar with them.

### Masking cards

The use of masking cards is a device that helps to focus children's attention on specific words or phrases and helps teaching 'that crucial eye-voice-ear link which makes print intelligible in the earliest stages of reading' (Don Holdaway, *The Foundations of Literacy*, 1979). Don Holdaway's work has become an established rationale for using Big Books which is at the very heart of teaching within the literacy hour.

The sliding mask allows the teacher to gradually reveal words or phrases that are to be focused on. These can be made in two ways, either as a sliding mask (which will require a sliding strip to be cut and a card loop fixed to the back to pull it through – see Figure 3a), or as a cut-out or 'fixed' mask which can be used to emphasize repeated phrases or refrains in a story (Figure 3b). Put Blu-tack on the back in order to fix the card to the page of text.

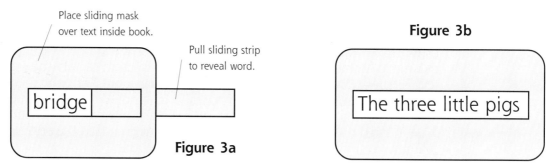

Place sliding mask over text inside book.

Pull sliding strip to reveal word.

bridge

**Figure 3a**

**Figure 3b**

The three little pigs

## GENERAL BOOK MAKING

A range of book-making activities is used in the units. Instructions for these are follows:

### Zigzag book

Cut a strip of thick paper or thin card. This can be half a sheet of A3 cut lengthwise or bigger or smaller as required. Make even folds in the paper to create a concertina effect (Figure 4). Extra zigzag strips can be joined on with adhesive tape if more pages are required.

**Figure 4**

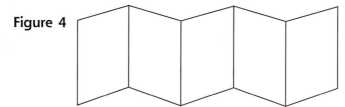

### Stapled book

Also known as 'little books', these are invaluable for story sequencing or story writing activities and can be made in different sizes and shapes. Start by working out how many pages are needed – remember that one folded sheet of paper will provide four pages. Take the appropriate number of sheets and fold each one exactly in half. Staple along the centre fold (Figure 5). To make a firmer cover, replace the outside sheet of paper with a piece of card. A laminated cover will help the book to last longer.

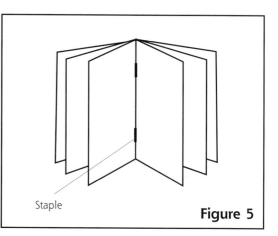

Staple

**Figure 5**

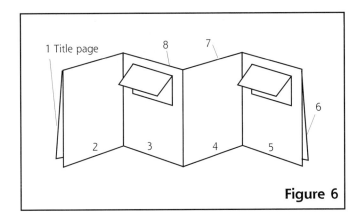

**Figure 6**

## Lift-the-flap book

Fold a sheet of A3 paper in half lengthways. Fold this in half widthways and in half again (Figure 6). Cut flaps carefully with a craft knife or sharp scissors on alternate pages, making a total of three flaps.

## Shape book

Make a card template of the shape you wish to use (keep the shape as simple as possible). Fold a sheet of card for the cover and enough cartridge paper to make the inside pages for one book, then use the template as an outline to cut through the whole book in one go (Figure 7a) and staple together.

Alternatively, you can make books with shaped covers only. To do this, trace round the template and cut several covers at once from card. Staple or sew each cover over the inside pages (Figure 7b).

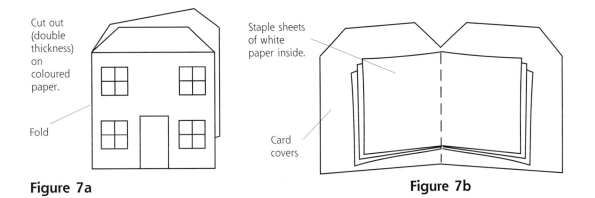

**Figure 7a**

**Figure 7b**

## USE OF AN OVERHEAD PROJECTOR

Having the use of an overhead projector (OHP) is ideal for whole-class work. Photocopiable texts and skills activities can then be copied onto acetate sheets to make overhead transparencies (OHTs) which can be projected onto a screen or a bare, white or light-coloured wall, or a whiteboard which can then be written on. Where an OHP is not available, photocopiable sheets should be enlarged to at least A3 size with 48-point text.

## INFORMATION AND COMPUTER TECHNOLOGY

■ For skills practice, using programs such as *Animated Alphabet*
■ For word processing, either by the teacher during shared or guided writing sessions, or by children using simpler word processing programmes, such as *Clicker Plus* (Crick Software) which enables the creation of grids similar to an overlay keyboard, but on screen
■ For creating own books and developing story writing using programs such as *StoryBook Weaver* (Iona Software)
■ For developing reading skills using interactive stories on CD ROM.

## A NOTE ON PHOTOCOPYING

Please note that where there is instruction to copy material from copyright texts, you need to ensure that this is done within the limits of the copying licence your school has. If children are using their own exercise books or paper for answers, then all photocopiable resources are re-usable.

# OVERVIEW: RECEPTION
## TERM 1

| UNIT | SPELLING/VOCABULARY | GRAMMAR/PUNCTUATION | COMPREHENSION/COMPOSITION |
|---|---|---|---|
| **HOUR 1** WRITING NON-FICTION Naming nonsense story. | Match names with the same initial letter. Write names using correct letter formation. Reinforce alphabet knowledge, using a computer program. | Know that names are written with capital letters at the beginning. Be able to compose alliterative sentences. | Take part in shared writing using names of pupils in the class. |
| **HOUR 5** READING FICTION AND POETRY Nursery rhymes. | Identify rhyming words. Explore onset and rimes -all, -ill, -ick, -ock, -et, -ay. Recognize initial letter sounds d, m and j. | Sequence words and sentences from familiar nursery rhymes using syntactical cueing. | Be able to read familiar nursery rhymes and follow the text when listening to taped versions. |
| **HOUR 1** READING FICTION AND POETRY *Little Lumpty* by Miko Imai. | Identify words that begin with the onset l. | Understand that words are ordered left to right. | Be able to recount the main points of a story in the correct sequence. Compare the story with the nursery rhyme 'Humpty Dumpty'. |
| **HOUR 5** READING NON-FICTION Simple non-fiction texts, including recounts. | Identify and understand the meaning of subject-specific vocabulary. Match key words. | Use awareness of the grammar of a sentence to predict words during shared reading. | Begin to distinguish between fiction and non-fiction. Know how to obtain information, and ask questions, from pictures. |
| **HOUR 5** WRITING NON-FICTION Alphabet books. | Know the letters of the alphabet and begin to learn alphabetical order. | Match upper case letters to lower case. | Be able to participate in shared and individual writing of ABC books. |
| **HOUR 5** READING FICTION AND POETRY Traditional tales. | Learn key words using cloze, tracking and posting games. | Know that words are ordered left to right and need to be read that way to make sense. | Recognize storybook language. Be able to locate and read parts of a text. Fit parts of a story into a structure. |

# OVERVIEW: RECEPTION
## TERM 1 (CONTINUED)

| UNIT | SPELLING/VOCABULARY | GRAMMAR/PUNCTUATION | COMPREHENSION/COMPOSITION |
|---|---|---|---|
| **HOUR 5** WRITING FICTION AND POETRY Traditional tales. | Explore rhyming sounds and spelling patterns of rime -*an*. Identify words beginning with *r*, *m* and c. Practise correct letter formation. | Write characters' names using capital letters. | Be able to take part in writing a class version of the story. Make individual books of the characters in the story. |
| **HOUR 2** READING NON-FICTION Notices and signs (Environmental print). | Use phonic and contextual cues to decipher new words. | Recognize capital letters and their corresponding lower case letters. | Recognize printed and handwritten words in a variety of settings. |
| **HOUR 3** WRITING NON-FICTION Notices and signs (Environmental print). | Write key words for use on signs and notices. | Write capital letters for use on signs and notices. | Be able to take part in shared writing of notices and directions. |

# OVERVIEW: RECEPTION
## TERM 2

| UNIT | SPELLING/VOCABULARY | GRAMMAR/PUNCTUATION | COMPREHENSION/ COMPOSITION |
|---|---|---|---|
| READING FICTION AND POETRY *Dear Zoo* by Rod Campbell. 'We've got a Wa Wa' by Rony Robinson. | Read key words in context. Develop phonological awareness through use of alliteration. Recognize rhyming words. | Match suitable adjectives to animals. | Read texts with a predictable structure and patterned language. Relate ideas in text to own experience. Understand and use correctly terms about books and print. |
| WRITING FICTION AND POETRY Stories with predictable structures and patterned language. | Collect words for word bank. Learn spellings of key words. Identify and write initial/ final phonemes in CVC words. | Use capital letters and full stops to demarcate sentences. | Shared writing of a class book entitled 'Dear Farm'. Emergent writing of letters. Make individual flap books. |
| READING NON-FICTION Simple non-fiction texts. | Identify key words. Understand the terms 'photograph', 'illustration' and 'caption'. | Match key words to sentences. Understand that a sentence should make sense. Ask questions and identify question marks. Use capital letter to start a sentence. | Read different non-fiction books on the theme of animals. Distinguish between a photograph and an illustration. Find information from photographs. |
| WRITING NON-FICTION Information books. | Be able to write own name and explore other words related to spelling of own name. | Write in sentences. Investigate the use of capital letters. | Make own information books including captions to pictures. |
| READING FICTION AND POETRY Counting rhymes and poems. | Explore number rhymes and rhyming words. | Use awareness of sentence structure to help sequence rhymes. | Read traditional, nursery and modern rhymes and poems. |
| WRITING FICTION AND POETRY Cumulative and repetitive poems: *Twinkle Twinkle Chocolate Bar* compiled by John Foster. | Find words with the c/k initial letter sound. Investigate onset and rimes (-ar, -at, -all, -ay). Identify letter patterns in words that rhyme. | Highlight repeated refrains. | Write shared poems substituting words and phrases from poems read. |

# OVERVIEW: RECEPTION
## TERM 2 (CONTINUED)

| UNIT | SPELLING/VOCABULARY | GRAMMAR/PUNCTUATION | COMPREHENSION/ COMPOSITION |
|---|---|---|---|
| **READING NON-FICTION** Simple non-fiction texts: Advertisements. | Identify and write initial and dominant phonemes in spoken words. Identify letter patterns in words. | Be aware of the use of capital letters for proper nouns. | Recognize printed and handwritten words in a variety of settings. Read words in advertisements. Locate print in the environment. Identify brand names. |
| **WRITING NON-FICTION** Lists, labels and sentences about food: *Don't Forget the Bacon!* by Pat Hutchins. | Match words to pictures on lists. Use packaging labels to copy words for lists. Consider the initial sounds of words. | Complete sentences using sentence frames. Use capital letters for proper nouns. | Write shopping lists. Complete sentences for favourite foods. Make posters. |

HOUR 5

HOUR 5

# OVERVIEW: RECEPTION
## TERM 3

| UNIT | SPELLING/VOCABULARY | GRAMMAR/PUNCTUATION | COMPREHENSION/ COMPOSITION |
|------|---------------------|---------------------|----------------------------|
| **HOUR 5** READING FICTION AND POETRY Stories with predictable structures and patterned language: *Each Peach Pear Plum* by Janet and Allan Ahlberg. | Develop 'book talk' vocabulary. Distinguish words that represent characters' names. Recognize key words. Locate rhyming words in a text. Generate words by analogy from rimes. | Understand that words are ordered from left to right and need to be read that way to make sense. Use awareness of grammar to fit in suitable missing words. Sequence sentences from the text. | Tell a story from pictures. Identify nursery rhyme characters. Match one spoken word to one written word. Take part in shared writing of alternative versions of the text. |
| **HOUR 1** READING NON-FICTION Simple non-fiction texts: Signs and labels. | Reinforce sight vocabulary of key words. | Find examples of capital letters and lower case letters. | Read signs and labels in the classroom. |
| **HOUR 5** READING NON-FICTION Recount: *My Day* by B. Wade. | Read high frequency words on sight. | Match upper and lower case letters. Identify full stops. | Sort fiction and non-fiction books. Predict contents from covers. Understand the sequence of events in a recount. |
| **HOUR 5** WRITING NON-FICTION Recounts: Our Class/All About Me. | Spell high frequency words, using visual features and spelling patterns. Link to handwriting practice. | Use capital letters appropriately, as for the start of names. | Through shared and guided writing, write simple recounts based on own experiences. |
| **HOUR 5** READING FICTION AND POETRY Stories with predictable structures and patterned language: 'Goldilocks and the Three Bears'. | Identify key words in the story. Match words with objects and pictures. | Use awareness of the grammar of a sentence to predict words. | Listen and retell a traditional story using story book language. Show an understanding of story structure. |
| **HOUR 5** WRITING FICTION AND POETRY Shape books: based on 'Goldilocks and the Three Bears'. | Recognize common spelling patterns. Collect words to describe characters. Practise correct letter formation. | Use capital letters and full stops to denote a sentence. | Use experience of stories as a basis for shared and independent writing. Write sentences to match pictures. Draw pictures to denote the structure of a story. Write letters using emergent writing. |
| **HOUR 1** READING FICTION AND POETRY Action rhymes. | Explore rhyming patterns. | Know that words are ordered left to right and need to be read that way to make sense. | Re-read and recite stories and rhymes with predictable and repeated patterns. Make one-to-one correspondences between written and spoken words. |

# OVERVIEW: RECEPTION
## TERM 3 (CONTINUED)

| | UNIT | SPELLING/VOCABULARY | GRAMMAR/PUNCTUATION | COMPREHENSION/COMPOSITION |
|---|---|---|---|---|
| HOUR 3 | READING NON-FICTION Simple non-fiction texts: *Toys* by Bobbie Neate. | Make a collection of topic-related words. Develop understanding of alphabetical order. | Use awareness of the grammar of a sentence to predict words when reading. | Understand and use correctly terms about books, such as cover, title, page and contents. Retrieve information from photographs and begin to devise appropriate questions. |
| HOUR 2 | WRITING NON-FICTION Simple non-fiction texts: A toy alphabet. | Identify and write initial and dominant phonemes in spoken words. | Expect written text to make sense and check for sense if it does not. | Begin to make notes from non-fiction books by drawing pictures. |
| HOUR 1 | READING FICTION AND POETRY Poetry with predictable structures and patterned language: 'The Slug's Trail' by Wendy Jolliffe. | Discriminate onsets from rimes using the *-ug* rime. Notice the effects of alliteration. | Highlight the use of capital letters in poems. | Be able to re-read and recite rhymes with predictable and repeated patterns and experiment with rhyming patterns. |

# PUPIL RECORD SHEET

| Pupil's name: | | | | Class | | Year group |
|---|---|---|---|---|---|---|
| Term | 1 | 2 | 3 | 1st half | | 2nd half |
| | | TARGET(S) | | INTERIM PROGRESS (inc. dates) | | ACHIEVEMENT AT END OF HALF TERM |
| Reading | | | | | | |
| Writing | | | | | | |

# Term 1

# NAMING NAMES

## OBJECTIVES

| UNIT | SPELLING/VOCABULARY | GRAMMAR/PUNCTUATION | COMPREHENSION/ COMPOSITION |
|---|---|---|---|
| WRITING NON-FICTION Naming nonsense story. | Match names with the same initial letter. Write names using correct letter formation. Reinforce alphabet knowledge, using a computer program. | Know that names are written with capital letters at the beginning. Be able to compose alliterative sentences. | Take part in shared writing using names of pupils in the class. |

## ORGANIZATION (1 HOUR)

| INTRODUCTION | WHOLE-CLASS SKILLS WORK | DIFFERENTIATED GROUP ACTIVITIES | CONCLUSION |
|---|---|---|---|
| Shared writing of alliterative sentences using pupils' names. Combine some of the sentences to make a nonsense story. | Reinforce correct letter formation and spelling during shared writing. Emphasize the use of a capital letter at the beginning of a name to show it is something important. | 1*: Shared writing of further sentences. 2: Pairs to work on computer using an alphabet program. Others to use magnetic letters to match letters in their names. Write and illustrate names. 3: Sort name cards with same first letter. | Discuss most common initial letter for pupils' names. Selected pupils from Group 1 share their sentences. |

## RESOURCES

Name cards for children in the class, board or flip chart, computer with an alphabet program (eg, *Animated Alphabet*, Sherston), magnetic or plastic letters, writing materials.

## PREPARATION

Make a name card (first names only) for each child and laminate them. You could add a picture to represent the sound the child's name begins with. Make sure the sound, as well as the letter, matches the picture – so the name 'Gemma' would need a picture of something beginning with the *j* sound, such as a giraffe.

### Introduction and whole-class skills work

Ask the children to sit in a circle holding their name cards. Next ask them to pass their name cards around the circle until you tell them to stop. They should then take turns to say the name on the card they are holding. If there is any confusion, use this as an opportunity to talk about the first letter on the card. Finally, ask the children to pass the cards back to their owners.

Now, work through the alphabet, asking them to stand up if their name begins with the letter A, B, and so on. Use letter names, but also refer to the sound they make. (If you have, for example, a Charlotte and a Catherine, this may be a good opportunity to point out that a letter does not always make the same sound.) Find out which is the most common letter at the start of their names.

Now tell them you are going to think of a silly sentence for someone's name, perhaps 'Harry hops home', or 'Susan slithers to school'. See if they can think of any other examples. Write some of the sentences on the board, or flip chart. Talk as you write, describing and reinforcing correct letter formation, and explaining that every name begins with a capital letter to show that names are important.

Hanif hops happily home.
Susan slithers sulkily to school.
Wendy walks each Wednesday.
Lucy loves licking lollies.
Carl's curls are cute.
Billy buys blue badges.
Deema drives a dinky Datsun.
Meera meets Mandy most mornings.

Using the sentences on the board, begin a nonsense story:
'Once upon a time silly Susan slithered into school where she met happy Harry...'
Ask the children to make suggestions for continuing the story, using names from the class, matched with words which have the same initial sound.

## Differentiated group activities

1*: Write alliterative sentences for each member of the group. Let the children take turns to make suggestions while you write the sentences on the board, or flip chart, for them all to see (again, reinforce correct letter formation). The group then re-reads the sentences.

2: Work in pairs, using an alphabet program, such as *Animated Alphabet*, on a computer. They should write and illustrate the first letter of their names by drawing objects that begin with the same letter, so 'Alison' might have an apple, ant, alligator or axe. Any members of the group without access to a computer should use plastic or magnetic letters to spell out the names of other children in their group.

3: Sort the class name cards into groups that begin with the same letter.

## Conclusion

Talk about the most common initial letters of the children's names. Count how many names in the class begin with the same letter and talk about whether they all sound the same (compare, for example, Christopher and Charlotte). Children from Group 1 can share some of the sentences they have made.

# NURSERY RHYMES

## OBJECTIVES

| UNIT | SPELLING/VOCABULARY | GRAMMAR/PUNCTUATION | COMPREHENSION/ COMPOSITION |
|---|---|---|---|
| READING FICTION AND POETRY Nursery rhymes. | Identify rhyming words. Explore onset and rimes -all, -ill, -ick, -ock, -et, -ay. Recognize initial letter sounds d, m and j. | Sequence words and sentences from familiar nursery rhymes using syntactical cueing. | Be able to read familiar nursery rhymes and follow the text when listening to taped versions. |

## ORGANIZATION (5 HOURS)

| | INTRODUCTION | WHOLE-CLASS SKILLS WORK | DIFFERENTIATED GROUP ACTIVITIES | CONCLUSION |
|---|---|---|---|---|
| HOUR 1 | Shared reading of 'Humpty Dumpty' emphasizing one-to-one matching. Oral cloze of rhyming words. Physical sequencing of parts of rhyme. | Highlight rhyming words. Use plastic letters to model onset and rime of 'fall/wall'. | 1*: Half read versions of Humpty rhyme. Others listen to taped rhymes (exchange). 2: Pair rhyming pictures. 3: Sequence pictures of Humpty Dumpty. | Selected pupils show matched rhyming pictures and sequenced versions of Humpty Dumpty. Shared reading of alternative versions of rhyme. Highlight rhyming words. |
| HOUR 2 | Shared reading of 'Hickory Dickory Dock'. Oral cloze of rhyming words. | Identify rhyming objects in a box. Play rhyming game 'I hear with my little ear a word that rhymes with…' | 1: Play 'Snap' using words and pictures with -ick and -ock rimes. 2*: Half the group read 'Hickory Dickory Dock'. Others listen to tape (exchange). 3: Sort and draw objects with -ock/-ick rimes. | Selected pupils show pictures of rhyming objects and examples of pictures/words with -ick and -ock rimes. Share nonsense versions of 'Hickory Dickory Dock'. Emphasize letter patterns. |
| HOUR 3 | Shared reading of 'Jack and Jill'. Re-enact the rhyme with different pupils' names to make alternative versions. | Match objects and words that begin with the sound j. Practise writing the letter. Demonstrate different onsets with rime -ill. | 1: Use plastic letters to make words using -ill rime. Play rhyming tracking game. 2: Draw pictures of words that begin with j. 3*: Guided reading of nursery rhyme Big Book with half the group. Underline rhyming words on acetate overlay. Others listen to nursery rhyme tape. | Selected pupils talk about words they made that rhyme with Jill, and pictures of words that begin with onset j. Go over alternative versions of 'Jack and Jill' with different pupils' names. |
| HOUR 4 | Shared reading of 'Little Miss Muffet'. Emphasize rhyming words. | Talk about words that begin with the same sound (alliteration). Play a memory game using words beginning with m. | 1*: Guided reading of nursery rhyme books with half the group. Others sequence lines from the rhyme (exchange). 2: Use plastic letters to make words with -et and -ay rimes. 3: Match nursery rhyme characters to objects. | Selected pupils show matched characters and objects and words made with -et and -ay rimes. Shared sequencing of lines using enlarged version of rhyme. |
| HOUR 5 | Shared reading of 'Hey Diddle Diddle'. Oral cloze of rhyming words. Physical sequencing of parts of rhyme. | Play lucky dip using an assortment of objects in a bag to see which ones begin with d sound. Match words to objects and practise writing the letter. | 1: Draw pictures of objects beginning with d and write words. 2: Play a rhyming tracking game. 3*: Sequence and read assorted rhymes (2 & 3 exchange tasks). | Selected pupils to show examples of objects beginning with d along with matched rhyming words and pictures. Play 'I hear with my little ear…' |

## RESOURCES

Big Book of nursery rhymes (which includes 'Humpty Dumpty', 'Little Miss Muffet', 'Hickory Dickory Dock', 'Jack and Jill', 'Hey Diddle Diddle'), acetate and non-permanent marker pen, plastic letters, nursery rhyme tape(s) and accompanying book(s), tape recorder and headphones, large sticky labels, computer and concept keyboard, picture dictionaries, writing and drawing materials.

Photocopiable pages 132 (Nursery rhyme sequencing cards from 'Each Peach, Pear Plum' unit, Term 3), 29 (Humpty Dumpty sequencing sheet), 30 and 31, (More Humpty Dumpties, and Even More Humpty Dumpties), 32 (Picture Cards: -ick and -ock rimes) and 33 (Who Needs What?).

Objects with names that rhyme with -ick and -ock in a box, objects that begin with a j sound and the corresponding words written on card, bag containing objects (some of which begin with the sound d), corresponding 'd' words on card to match these objects, rhyming tracking board game (see page 27), dice.

## PREPARATION

Copy photocopiable page 132 (Sequencing nursery rhymes from 'Each Peach, Pear, Plum' unit, Term 3) and make one set of cards by colouring, cutting and laminating. Make a second enlarged set in the same way. Photocopy enough Humpty Dumpty sequencing sheets (photocopiable page 29) for Group 3.

Make enlarged copies of photocopiable pages 30 and 31 (alternative versions of Humpty Dumpty). Copy two sets of the -ick and -ock rimes Picture Cards (photocopiable page 32); one will be used to make the tracking game, the other for a game of 'Snap'. Write the words on the reverse of the 'Snap' set and laminate them.

Make a rhyming tracking game by using the rhyming pictures from photocopiable page 32). Colour the pictures and stick them onto a board at random (see diagram on page 27). Laminate the board.

Make enlarged versions of photocopiable page 33 (Who Needs What?) for Group 3 in Hour 4.

Make enlarged versions of a selection of nursery rhymes, including 'Hickory Dickory Dock', 'Jack and Jill', 'Little Miss Muffet' and 'Hey Diddle Diddle', by typing onto a computer using 48-point font size. Photocopy one set of these and laminate them. Cut another copy of each into separate lines.

### Introduction

Introduce a Big Book of nursery rhymes. Discuss the cover and ask the children which nursery rhymes they can remember, then read selected examples, including 'Humpty Dumpty'. Bring out the nursery rhyme sequencing cards and ask three children to physically sequence the cards by standing up and holding them, then getting into the correct order.

### Whole-class skills work

Read 'Humpty Dumpty' again, pausing for the children to provide the rhyming words 'wall/fall' and 'men/again'. Place a sheet of acetate over the Big Book and, with a non-permanent marker pen, underline the words that rhyme. Then, using plastic letters, show how 'wall' can be changed into 'fall'. Ask the children if they can think of any other examples of rhyming words.

### Differentiated group activities

1*: With half of the group, carry out a guided read of the Big Book of nursery rhymes, concentrating on 'Humpty Dumpty'. Then read the alternative versions of Humpty Dumpty on the enlarged copies of photocopiable pages 30 and 31, emphasizing rhyming words. Meanwhile, the rest of the group should listen to the tape of nursery rhymes and follow them in the book. The children can exchange tasks after about 10 minutes.

2: Use the rhyming pictures from photocopiable page 32 and match those that rhyme.

3: Sequence the pictures of nursery rhymes (from photocopiable page 132) that are already cut up and laminated. The children may also colour, cut up and sequence their own Humpty Dumpty rhyme (pictures from photocopiable page 29).

## Conclusion

Ask some of the children from Group 2 to show examples of rhyming pictures that match. Group 3 can also show their sequenced nursery rhymes. Children from Group 1 should talk about the alternative versions of 'Humpty Dumpty' before you read some of these together. Ask the children to suggest others, emphasizing the rhyming words.

## Introduction

Begin with a shared reading of 'Hickory Dickory Dock', using either a nursery rhyme Big Book or enlarged card version. Stress the rhyming words as you read. Now read the rhyme again but pause at the rhyming words and ask the children to suggest the word that fits. You might also consider reading it again, this time putting in words that obviously do *not* fit the rhyme to highlight the effect that rhyme has (perhaps 'Hickory Dickory Dock, the mouse ran up the wall').

## Whole-class skills work

Bring out the box in which you have a number of rhyming objects (such as clock, sock, block), take the objects out one at a time and ask the children to identify them. (You could later display these in the classroom with the corresponding words on card.) Play a rhyming game, such as: 'I hear with my little ear a word that rhymes with... sock'. If any children find this difficult you can provide added clues, perhaps: 'I hear with my little ear a word that rhymes with sock, and could be somebody at the door'.

## Differentiated group activities

1: Play a game of 'Snap' with pictures that rhyme with *-ick* and *-ock* (from photocopiable page 32). As an extension the children might try using just the words, which should be on the back of the pictures.

2*: Half of the group should read 'Hickory Dickory Dock' with the teacher and then make up alternative versions, using nonsense words such as 'Pickory, Tickory Sock'. Use plastic letters to show that it is the first letter each time which changes. The rest of the group, meanwhile, should listen to nursery rhymes on tape, following the words in the book(s). Exchange tasks after about 10 minutes.

3: Sort the rhyming objects into sets of *-ock* and *-ick* rimes. Provide an A4 page, divided into two, one side headed 'ick', the other 'ock'. Ask the children to draw objects that rhyme with each rime under the correct headings.

## Conclusion

Ask a few of the children to show the pictures of the rhyming objects they have drawn and examples of the pictures and words that rhyme with *-ick* and *-ock*. Share the nonsense versions of 'Hickory Dickory Dock' and write some of the words on the board to emphasize the letter patterns.

## Introduction

Start with a shared reading of 'Jack and Jill' using a Big Book of nursery rhymes or an enlarged card version. Choose two children to re-enact the rhyme while the rest of the class recites it. Now choose two other children, preferably with names that both begin with the same sound (Kelly and Kim, for example). Write their names on large sticky labels and stick these onto their backs (or you could write the names on card and hang these around their necks). Ask the children to help you make up a different version of Jack and Jill – 'Kelly and Kim were going to see Jim', or 'Jason and Jane went down the lane'. If possible use examples that share the same letter pattern as well as rhyming orally (not 'Jane' and 'rain').

## Whole-class skills work

Introduce the collection of objects that begin with the sound *j* and the corresponding word cards. Encourage the children to match the words to the objects. (You may like to point out that this sound can be made by different letters, as 'g' in 'giant'.) Practise the correct letter formation for the letter *j*, both upper and lower case. Some children might practise on the board or flip chart, while others could try skywriting. Show the children how to write the name 'Jill' and point out that by changing the first letter the word can be changed.

### Differentiated group activities

1: Use plastic letters to make different words which use the -*ill* rime. Then let pairs of children practise identifying -*ick* and -*ock* rhymes by playing the rhyming tracking game. Each child, in turn, throws a dice and moves a coloured counter around the track. As he or she lands on a picture he or she must say the name of the object depicted and then, if this is done correctly, move to another picture that shows a rhyming object. The child who reaches the finish first is the winner. You could make this more difficult by adding more rhyming pictures.

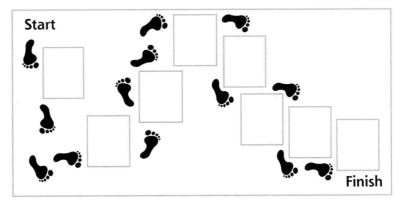

2: Draw pictures of words that begin with *j* with the help of simple picture dictionaries. Any children who are able might add the words.
3*: Half of the group read the nursery rhyme Big Book with the teacher, underlining rhyming words on a sheet of acetate over the book. The rest of the group listen to nursery rhymes on tape, following these in the book. Exchange tasks after about 10 minutes.

### Conclusion

Ask a few children to talk about words they made that rhyme with 'Jill', while others show their pictures of words that begin with the onset *j*. Reinforce alternative versions of 'Jack and Jill' using the names of children in the class.

### Introduction

Begin with a shared reading of 'Little Miss Muffet' using the Big Book of nursery rhymes or an enlarged card version. Emphasize any rhyming words.

### Whole-class skills work

Talk about words that begin with the same sound as 'Miss Muffet' and ask the children if they can think of other words which begin with the *m* sound. Emphasize this by reading a tongue twister, or by playing the memory game – 'I went to market and I bought milk, mincemeat, marshmallows...' Each child has to try to remember, and repeat, what other children have said, then add something else that begins with *m*.

### Differentiated group activities

1*: Half the group should carry out a guided read of small versions of nursery rhyme books with the teacher, while the rest of the group sequence lines from the rhyme using the enlarged, cut-up and laminated versions (see 'Preparation', page 25). One or two children could use the computer and concept keyboard for this with an overlay. Exchange tasks after about 10 minutes.
2: Use plastic letters to make words with -*et* and -*ay* rimes. Provide some examples to help. Children should write a list of the words they make.
3: Match nursery characters to associated objects using enlarged copies of the pictures on photocopiable page 33. The children should cut out and stick the character and object next to each other.

### Conclusion

Ask a number of children to show the matched characters, or the objects and words made with -*et* and -*ay* rimes. Use an enlarged version of the rhyme which has been cut up into separate lines to carry out shared sequencing of lines. Emphasize that the position of the rhyming words will help the children to order the lines correctly.

**HOUR 5**

### Introduction
Begin with a shared reading of 'Hey Diddle Diddle'. Then re-read the rhyme, pausing before the rhyming words so that the children can fill them in. Physically sequence the rhyme using enlarged rhyming cards, as in Hour 1.

### Whole-class skills work
Play lucky dip with an assortment of objects in a bag, checking to see which ones begin with the *d* sound. Using words on card, ask a few of the children to match objects to words. Practise letter formation using skywriting, with some children demonstrating on the board or flip chart.

### Differentiated group activities
1: Draw pictures of objects beginning with *d* and write the words, using simple picture dictionaries.
2: Play the rhyming tracking game (see Hour 3).
3*: Work with the teacher to sequence and read assorted rhymes.
(Groups 2 and 3 exchange tasks after about 10 minutes.)

### Conclusion
Ask some of the children to show examples of objects beginning with *d* and matched rhyming pictures. Play another game of 'I hear with my little ear...'.

# HUMPTY DUMPTY

Humpty Dumpty had a great fall.

Couldn't put Humpty together again.

All the King's horses and all the King's men,

Humpty Dumpty sat on a wall.

# MORE HUMPTY DUMPTIES

Humpty Dumpty sat on a box.
Humpty Dumpty saw a fox.

Humpty Dumpty sat on a chair.
Humpty Dumpty combed his hair.

Humpty Dumpty sat in a tree.
Humpty Dumpty saw a bee.

Humpty Dumpty sat on a log.
Humpty Dumpty saw a dog.

# EVEN MORE HUMPTY DUMPTIES!

Humpty Dumpty sat on a wall.
Humpty Dumpty had a great fall.
All the King's horses and all the King's men,

Trod on him!

Humpty Dumpty sat on a wall.
Humpty Dumpty had a great fall.
All the King's men didn't know what to do,
So one went to fetch a tub of glue.

# PICTURE CARDS: -ICK AND -OCK RIMES

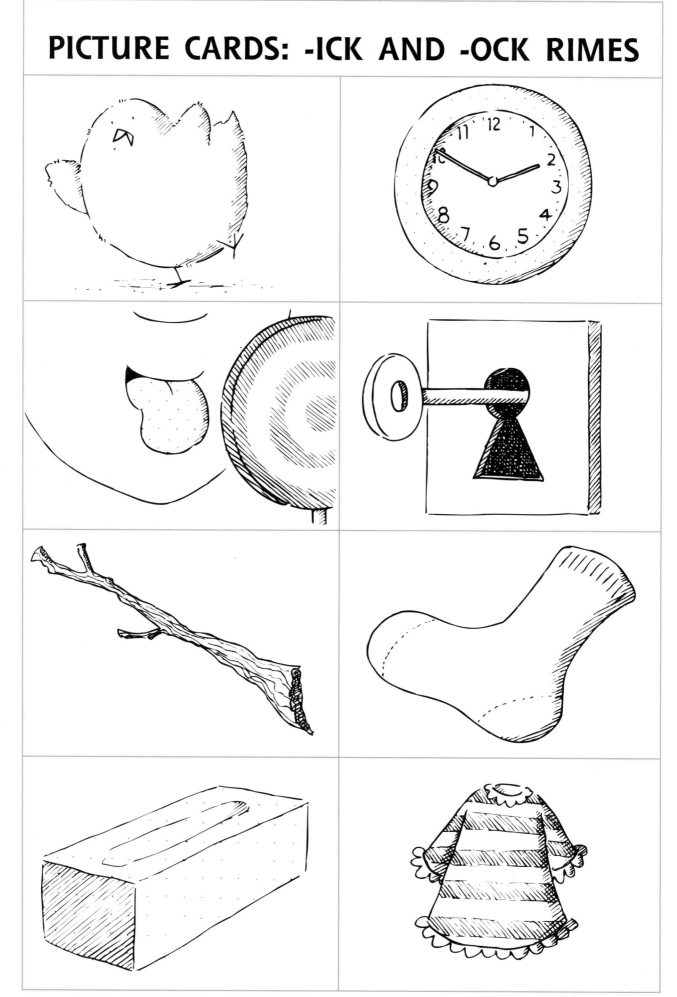

# WHO NEEDS WHAT?

Humpty Dumpty

bowl and spoon

mouse

wall

Jack and Jill

fiddle

Little Miss Muffet

clock

cat

bucket

# LITTLE LUMPTY

## OBJECTIVES

| UNIT | SPELLING/VOCABULARY | GRAMMAR/PUNCTUATION | COMPREHENSION/ COMPOSITION |
|---|---|---|---|
| READING FICTION AND POETRY *Little Lumpty* by Miko Imai. | Identify words that begin with the onset *l*. | Understand that words are ordered left to right. | Be able to recount the main points of a story in the correct sequence. Compare the story with the nursery rhyme 'Humpty Dumpty'. |

## ORGANIZATION (1 HOUR)

| | INTRODUCTION | WHOLE-CLASS SKILLS WORK | DIFFERENTIATED GROUP ACTIVITIES | CONCLUSION |
|---|---|---|---|---|
| HOUR 1 | Read the story of *Little Lumpty*. Use enlarged extracts of the text to compare with the nursery rhyme 'Humpty Dumpty'. | Look at examples of alliteration and words beginning with *l* in the text. Reinforce with objects beginning with *l* and practise correct letter formation. | 1: Draw pictures to sequence the beginning, middle and end of the story. 2: Draw pictures and write words that begin with *l*. 3*: Guided read with half the group, while the rest look for words beginning with *l* in extracts of the text (exchange). | Selected pupils show examples of pictures and words beginning with *l*. Pupils from Group 1 retell the story of Little Lumpty using their pictures of the beginning, middle and end of the story. Invent tongue-twisters. |

## RESOURCES

Copies of *Little Lumpty* by Miko Imai (Walker Books, ISBN 0-7445-3605-7) – ideally enough for half the children in Group 3, photocopiable pages 36 (Little Lumpty) and 37 (L Pictures), a selection of objects, or pictures of objects, that begin with the letter *l*, a Big Book of nursery rhymes including 'Humpty Dumpty', A3 paper, board or flip chart, picture dictionaries, writing materials.

## PREPARATION

Make enough copies of photocopiable page 36 for each child in Group 3. Divide A3 paper into three sections widthways for Group 1. Make a copy of photocopiable page 37 for Group 2.

## STORY SYNOPSIS

This is a story based on the nursery rhyme 'Humpty Dumpty'. Little Lumpty is a similar egg-shaped character who dreams of climbing Humpty Dumpty's famous wall. The story describes how he does climb it, but gets stuck and has to be rescued.

### Introduction

Introduce the picture book *Little Lumpty*. Talk about the cover of the book and read the title. Ask the children to predict what it is about. Can they tell from the picture or the title? Then read the back-cover blurb and ask the children what that tells them about the story (that it is based on the nursery rhyme 'Humpty Dumpty'). Look at the inscription 'In memory of Humpty Dumpty' and discuss what it means. Read the story with expression and enjoyment, possibly stopping occasionally to ask the children to predict what is going to happen (perhaps when Little Lumpty is on the top of the wall). When you have read it through, compare the story with the original nursery rhyme. Talk about what sort of character Lumpty was, and ask the children what they liked about the story.

## Whole-class skills work

Talk about the letters at the beginning of 'Little' and 'Lumpty' and what sound the letter makes. Look through the book for words that begin with *l* and write them on the board or flip chart. Now show the children a selection of objects that begin with *l* (for example, a lamp, a picture of a ladder). Say what they are, emphasizing the *l* sound and demonstrate the correct formation of the letter as you write the words on the board or flip chart. The children can practise by skywriting while a few demonstrate on the board or flip chart.

## Differentiated group activities

1: Sequence the story on a sheet of A3 paper which has been divided into three sections and has been headed 'Little Lumpty'. If a line is ruled across the bottom of the page this will leave a small margin that the teacher or children can write in later. Explain that they should first draw the beginning of the story, then the end of the story and, finally, what happened in the middle. Children often find this an easier way to sequence a story than working in strict order.

```
+-----------------------------------+
|         | Little Lumpty |         |
|         |               |         |
|         |               |         |
|         |               |         |
|         |               |         |
|         |               |         |
|-----------------------------------|
|                                   |
+-----------------------------------+
```

2: Provide the group with photocopiable page 37 (to use as a model) and A4 paper. Ask them to draw their own pictures of and write the words for, objects beginning with the sound 'l'. Provide picture dictionaries to help them find further words for this.
3*: Half of the group read the story with the teacher (preferably with one copy of the book each). The others highlight words beginning with *l* on photocopied extracts of the text (photocopiable page 36). Exchange tasks after about 10 minutes.

## Conclusion

Ask a few children from Group 2 to show their pictures of objects beginning with *l*. Group 1 children should re-tell the story using the sequenced pictures. Finish by asking the class to help you make up a tongue twister of words beginning with *l*, along the lines of 'Little Lumpty loved long ladders.'

# LITTLE LUMPTY

In the little town of Dumpty there was a high wall. Humpty Dumpty had fallen from it long, long ago. But people still remembered him.

Every day children played by the wall and sang,

"Humpty Dumpty sat on the wall.

Humpty Dumpty had a great fall."

Little Lumpty loved the wall and always

dreamed about climbing to the top.

"Don't ever do that," Lumpty's mother

said.

"Remember, all the King's horses and all

the King's men

couldn't put Humpty Dumpty together

again."

But Little Lumpty couldn't stop thinking

about the wall.

One day, on his way home from school,

he found a long ladder and dragged it to

the wall.  He climbed up ... and up ...

and up.

# L PICTURES

# INTRODUCING NON-FICTION

## OBJECTIVES

| UNIT | SPELLING/VOCABULARY | GRAMMAR/PUNCTUATION | COMPREHENSION/ COMPOSITION |
|---|---|---|---|
| READING NON-FICTION Simple non-fiction texts, including recounts. | Identify and understand the meaning of subject-specific vocabulary. Match key words. | Use awareness of the grammar of a sentence to predict words during shared reading. | Begin to distinguish between fiction and non-fiction. Know how to obtain information, and ask questions, from pictures. |

## ORGANIZATION (5 HOURS)

| | INTRODUCTION | WHOLE-CLASS SKILLS WORK | DIFFERENTIATED GROUP ACTIVITIES | CONCLUSION |
|---|---|---|---|---|
| HOUR 1 | Whole-class shared reading of a non-fiction Big Book. Compare covers of fiction and non-fiction books to spot differences and consider types of pictures. | Match captions to pictures on a Big Book. | 1: Work in pairs to fix labels to a diagram or picture. 2*: Half the group read a Big Book, looking at captions. Others locate books with photographs (exchange). 3: Make a simple non-fiction book cover. | Selected pupils from Groups 1 & 3 show examples of their work. Emphasize the difference between fiction and non-fiction. |
| HOUR 2 | Whole-class shared reading, comparing fiction and non-fiction by doing a 'picture flick'. Ask questions about some of the pictures – 'read a picture'. | Identify book titles – matching titles to books. | 1*: Guided reading of a Big Book, then ask questions from pictures. Others sort fiction and non-fiction books (exchange). 2: Make a simple non-fiction book cover. 3: Play key words game. | Group 1 children show a picture and ask an appropriate question. Emphasize that information is often given by pictures. Look at examples of book covers. |
| HOUR 3 | Shared reading of a non-fiction Big Book. Highlight differences between photographs and drawings. | Look at vocabulary to ensure that subject-specific words in non-fiction book are understood. Make a word bank of subject-specific words (perhaps to do with animals). | 1: Make book covers using magazines photographs. 2: Library role play, looking for books on a topic. 3*: Guided reading to identify words previously highlighted. Others select books containing photographs (exchange). | Re-emphasize the difference between photographs and drawings. Show examples of book covers with photographs. |
| HOUR 4 | Shared reading of a non-fiction book to demonstrate that we only read the parts of a non-fiction book that interest us. | Point to words as they are read to emphasize the one-to-one matching of the spoken to the written word. | 1*: Half the group read an extract from a non-fiction book. Others sequence sentences (exchange). 2: Sequence pictures. 3: Library role play. | Selected pupils talk about chosen extracts. Discuss how these were chosen. Show examples of sequencing pictures. Show examples of non-fiction books form library. |
| HOUR 5 | Shared reading of extracts from fiction and non-fiction books. Discuss differences. | Identify high frequency words using masking card. | 1: Library role play. 2*: Half the group read a non-fiction book. Others listen to a tape of a non-fiction book (exchange). 3: Track key words on newspapers or magazines. | Selected pupils show examples of key words matched to text. Re-read Big Book sentences containing key words. Choose a non-fiction book from the class library. |

## RESOURCES

Non-fiction Big Book, small non-fiction books and several examples of fiction Big Books.

A selection of large pictures or diagram with appropriate labels mounted onto card or laminated (these could be photocopied from a non-fiction book, bearing in mind that only one copy of a published text can be made for classroom use), a large poster on any non-fiction topic which can be used for labelling (see Preparation, below).

Photocopiable pages 43 (Make Your Own Book Cover), 44 (Put the Pictures in Order), 45 (Parts of the Body) and 46 (Parts of an Animal), a selection of pictures from magazines on similar themes, including photographs.

Writing materials, including pencils, crayons, a yellow felt-tipped pen, Post-it notes, blank cards, masking card, glue sticks, Blu-Tack.

Labelled boxes or baskets for sorting books into fiction and non-fiction, library props for role play, such as a date stamp or an index card to list the titles of books, taped extract from a non-fiction book (home-made or commercially recorded) with several copies of the relevant book, newspaper and magazine extracts.

## PREPARATION

Photocopy sufficient blank book covers (photocopiable page 43) for the whole class. Cover the labels on the large poster, writing out the words from the labels onto card. Prepare several different labelled diagrams by covering the labels, possibly with a Post-it note. Write out the missing labels from the diagrams on card. Blank out the titles on a fiction and non-fiction book. Write out the titles, in large print, on card.

Photocopy the selection of sequencing pictures (photocopiable page 44), then laminate and cut them up. Make an enlarged copy of photocopiable page 45 and enough copies of photocopiable pages 45 and 46 for Group 1.

Write or type separate sentences from a non-fiction book on A4 paper and photocopy sufficient for Group 1. Choose key words relevant to the non-fiction Big Book you have selected and write these out on cards, making two sets.

### Introduction

Begin by looking at an enlarged (Big Book) non-fiction book. Talk about the book cover and ask the children to predict what it is about from the title and the pictures. Read the blurb on the back, if there is one, and talk about the kind of book they think it is. Flick through the pages, looking at the pictures, and explain that, as you do not have time to read the whole book, you are going to choose a part to read.

Read the chosen section, still looking at the pictures, then ask for any comments. You could ask if it sounds like a story.

Next look at the cover of a fiction Big Book. (Try to find an example of one that is obviously about fictional characters, for example, one with illustrations of fairy tale characters). Ask the children to say what they think is different about this book. Help them to understand that non-fiction books often use photographs, but fiction books usually have illustrations. Ensure the children understand the difference between 'photograph' and 'illustration'.

### Whole-class skills work

Look further at photographs in a non-fiction Big Book and read the captions. Then, using the poster with blanked-out spaces for labels, or an enlarged version of photocopiable page 45, read out the missing labels and ask different children to work out where they should go. Attach them in position with Blu-Tack.

### Differentiated group activities

1: Work in pairs to add the missing labels to the prepared pictures or diagrams. (If possible, try to provide two or three different examples, such as the parts of a bicycle or a car.) Photocopiable pages 45 (parts of the body) or 46 (parts of an animal) could be used for this activity.

2*: Guided reading of the non-fiction Big Book with half of the group, looking at the captions to the pictures. The others sort a selection of books, making a pile of those which contain photographs. Exchange tasks after about 10 minutes.

3: Make a simple non-fiction book cover (see photocopiable page 43). This needs to include a title (which could be written in advance by the teacher in yellow felt-tipped pen for the child to trace over), their name and a photograph cut out from a magazine and stuck on. Children need to ensure that the title of their book and the photograph match. If time allows, they can draw another appropriate picture on the back cover, then seek adult help to write the caption later.

### Conclusion

Children from the different groups should be asked to show examples of pictures with labels and examples of book covers they have made. Discuss the subject of the books and if they will be fiction or non-fiction. Reiterate the differences.

### Introduction

Begin with a whole-class shared reading of a non-fiction Big Book (it can be the same one used in Hour 1) and a fiction Big Book. Look at both book covers and discuss (if they are books that have not been used before, ask the children to predict the subject matter). Do a 'picture flick' of both books and talk about the contents. Now focus on a photograph in the non-fiction book and ask the children to talk about it. Discuss the type of questions that might be asked about the photograph, using question words such as: '**what** is happening?'; '**why** are they doing that?'; '**where** are they?'.

### Whole-class skills work

Use a different non-fiction book with the title blanked (perhaps with a Post-it note). Ask the children to use the picture and the blurb to guess what the title might be. Do the same with a fiction book, then show the children the two separate titles on card. Ask the class to help you read them and talk about some of the words, starting with what letter/ sound they begin with. Ask a few individual children to choose which title fits which book. Then display the books and titles matched.

### Differentiated group activities

1*: Guided reading, with half of the group, of the non-fiction Big Book, looking at the pictures and asking questions about them. The rest of the group sort a selection of fiction and non-fiction books into appropriately labelled baskets or boxes. Exchange tasks after 10 minutes.
2: Make a non-fiction book cover using photocopiable page 43 (as in Hour 1).
3: Play a pairs/matching game using the prepared sets of key words.

### Conclusion

Children from Group 1 should show examples of non-fiction books with photographs. Re-emphasize that pictures too can be read if we ask and answer a relevant question about them. Group 2 children might show their non-fiction book covers and challenge the rest of the class to guess what the book is about from the picture.

### Introduction

Remind the class that we usually only read parts of a non-fiction book and ask them to help select a part, using a Big Book (this could be the one used in Hours 1 and 2, but select a different part). Look for photographs and drawings, highlighting the differences.

### Whole-class skills work

Look at key vocabulary associated with the book (names of animals, for example) and ensure that specific words are understood. Include the words in a class word bank, which could have pictures (of animals) and words on card. Display these on a wall with Blu-Tack so that children can use them to check when they are working.

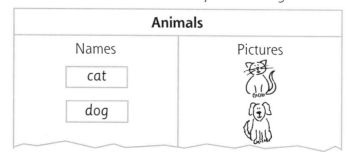

### Differentiated group activities

1: Make non-fiction book covers (as in Hours 1 and 2). The children will need to select photographs from magazines to stick onto the cover. They could add further pictures inside and write corresponding words.

2: Carry out a library role play in the class library or book corner. One child acts as the librarian, while the others look for books that contain photographs of… (provide a list with words and pictures on as in the class word bank). Props such as library cards or date stamps will add to the authenticity. (A visit to the local library, or from a librarian who could come into school, would be of great help, especially to any children who have no experience of public libraries.)

3*: Guided reading with the teacher to identify words previously highlighted on the class word bank, with half the group, while the rest select books that contain photographs. Exchange tasks after about 10 minutes.

### Conclusion

Select some Group 1 children to show their book covers with photographs. Reiterate the difference between drawings and photographs, and show a few examples. Choose one child to visit the class library and select a non-fiction book.

**HOUR 4**

### Introduction

Begin with a whole-class shared reading of a non-fiction Big Book to demonstrate that we only read the parts of a non-fiction book which interest us. (This could again be the same book used in Hours 1, 2 and 3, if a different section is chosen.) Discuss with the class the information obtained from the corresponding photographs.

### Whole-class skills work

Use a pointer to point to each word as it is read to emphasize how one spoken word matches one written word. This will also reinforce the direction of print. Choose children who need help with this to take turns at pointing as you read.

### Differentiated group activities

1*: Guided reading of an extract chosen from a non-fiction book with half the group (this can be with either the Big Book, or sets of smaller books if enough are available). The children should all point as the teacher reads first, then again later as they read individually (if the text is too difficult, individuals can read with the teacher). The rest of the group work in pairs to match words on card to the prepared sentences from a non-fiction book, then read the complete sentence. Exchange tasks after about 10 minutes

2: Work on sequencing tasks using sets of sequencing pictures (either your own, such as a chicken hatching out of an egg, or those on photocopiable page 44). The children need to arrange the pictures in the correct order. This can be made more difficult by mixing two or more sets of sequencing pictures.

3: Group role play in the class library as in Hour 3.

### Conclusion

Ask a few children from Group 1 to choose an extract from a non-fiction book to talk about, then say why they chose that extract. Show the sequencing pictures, talking about the information contained in each set and discussing the correct order. Group 3 children should show examples of books they found in the class library.

**HOUR 5**

**INTRODUCING NON-FICTION**

### Introduction

Begin with whole-class shared reading of extracts from a non-fiction Big Book and a fiction Big Book. Discuss with the children the ways in which they are different.

### Whole-class skills work

Using examples of high frequency key words on card, appropriate to the book you have chosen, ask different children to identify the words in the Big Book. Read the sentence in which the word(s) are contained to the class. Then, using a card mask with a sliding strip (see main Introduction, page 12), reveal one word at a time and read the complete sentence.

### Differentiated group activities

1: Role play in the class library (as in Hours 3 and 4). Pupils might be asked to write the names of non-fiction books on index cards and ensure that they are matched to the appropriate books.

2*: Guided reading of a non-fiction Big Book (or sets of smaller books if enough are available) with half the group. Children identify high frequency words and try to read the sentences which contain them. Offer further practice of masking words to help to develop context cues. Meanwhile the rest of the group should listen to an extract of a non-fiction book on tape, with one copy of the text between two. Exchange tasks after about 10 minutes.

3: Track key words, which were identified during the whole-class skills work, on a page from a newspaper or a magazine. Highlight or underline the key words.

### Conclusion

A few children might show examples of key words matched to text or found in newspapers or magazines. Use masking card on a Big Book to highlight key words and re-read sentences, encourage the children to predict, using their grammatical awareness. Selected Group 1 children should choose a non-fiction book from the class library and read the corresponding title on the index card.

# MAKE YOUR OWN BOOK COVER

by

■ Front: Fill in the title, add a picture and the name of the author.

■ Back: Draw a picture in the box.

# PUT THE PICTURES IN ORDER

# PARTS OF THE BODY

| eye | head | ear |
|---|---|---|
| nose | shoulder | arm |
| finger | hand | knee |
| toe | leg | foot |

# PARTS OF AN ANIMAL

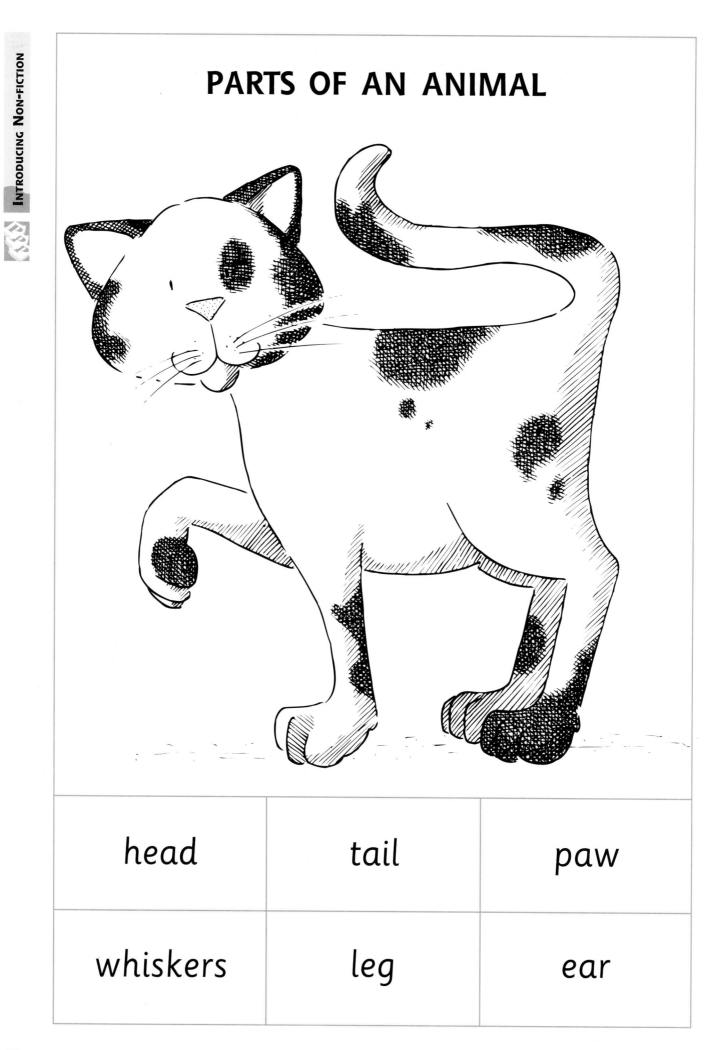

| head | tail | paw |
|---|---|---|
| whiskers | leg | ear |

# ALPHABET BOOKS

## OBJECTIVES

| UNIT | SPELLING/VOCABULARY | GRAMMAR/PUNCTUATION | COMPREHENSION/ COMPOSITION |
|------|---------------------|---------------------|----------------------------|
| WRITING NON-FICTION Alphabet books. | Know the letters of the alphabet and begin to learn alphabetical order. | Match upper case letters to lower case. | Be able to participate in shared and individual writing of ABC books. |

## ORGANIZATION (5 HOURS)

| | INTRODUCTION | WHOLE-CLASS SKILLS WORK | DIFFERENTIATED GROUP ACTIVITIES | CONCLUSION |
|---|--------------|-------------------------|--------------------------------|------------|
| HOUR 1 | Introduce alphabet books using a large ABC book. Discuss pictures and words for each page. | Shared writing of a page for class ABC book. | 1: Use large cut-out letter to find and stick pictures of objects beginning with that letter. 2*: Shared writing of words beginning with same letter. 3: Pairs use alphabet program, while others use 'alphabet box'. | Selected pupils show their cut-out letters with pictures and examples of drawings and corresponding words. Finish by singing the alphabet song. |
| HOUR 2 | Shared reading of large ABC book. Look at other examples of ABC books on different themes (see Resources, below). | Play 'I spy with my little eye something beginning with…'. | 1*: Shared writing of words beginning with same letter. 2: Pairs use alphabet program, while others use 'alphabet box'. 3. Listen to alphabet songs on tape. | Selected pupils show examples of their work. Play 'I spy'… to finish. |
| HOUR 3 | Shared reading of examples of ABC books. Shared writing of further examples for class ABC book. | Make a washing line of letters of the alphabet, matching upper and lower case letters. | 1: Make individual ABC books. Recognize lower and upper case letters 2: Work with large cut-out letters to stick pictures of matching objects. 3*: Shared writing of words beginning with same letter. | Pupils show examples of individual books. Read further examples of page(s) from class Big Book. Sing alphabet song. |
| HOUR 4 | Shared reading of ABC books. | Put letters, pictures and pupils' names in correct place in class ABC Big Book. Demonstrate use of class index box. | 1*: Make ABC index box. 2: Work on individual ABC books. 3: Hunt the letter – look for letters to stick onto chart. | Group 3 pupils show their charts of letters. Discuss the differences in typeface. Show examples of individual ABC index cards. Make an 'alphabet sun'. |
| HOUR 5 | Shared reading of class big ABC book. | Ring capital letters on laminated ABC book, or acetate overlay. | 1: Hunt the letter – look for letters to stick onto chart. Make lists of words beginning with letter. 2*: Continue work on ABC index box. 3: Work on individual ABC books. | Selected pupils show individual ABC books and examples of 'hunt the letter' work. Play a class game of 'Snap' with lower and upper case letters. |

## RESOURCES

A big ABC book, a selection of smaller alphabet books, examples of ABC books on different themes, eg, *Alfie's Alphabet* by Shirley Hughes (Red Fox ISBN 0-09-922042-3), picture dictionaries, photocopiable pages 52–54.

Large alphabet letters, plastic or wooden upper and lower case letters, objects which begin with different letters of the alphabet, or magazines with pictures of objects for different letters of the alphabet (photocopiable pages 52–54 could be used for this), a box containing assorted alphabet items such as games, puzzles, a range of alphabet books or mounted alphabet cards with picture clues, a second box or bag.

Alphabet song on tape, tape recorder and headphones, computer and alphabet program such as *Animated Alphabet* (Sherston).

Writing materials including: small, unlined exercise books, A4-size card, scissors, glue sticks, a small box (a plastic index box is ideal) with cards and alphabet index cards, a large sheet of acetate and non-permanent marker pens, a flip chart with large sheets of paper, drawing and painting materials.

A washing line made from strong string or nylon, upper and lower case alphabet letters on card, pegs.

## PREPARATION

Make enough copies of photocopiable pages 52–54 (Alphabet Pictures) for the whole class. Make alphabet cards by printing or writing upper and lower case letters in the middle of A4-size card, then putting pictures of objects beginning with the same letter around (some of the pictures from photocopiable pages 52–54 could be used for this) and writing the words underneath (see Figure 2). These could be laminated for extended use.

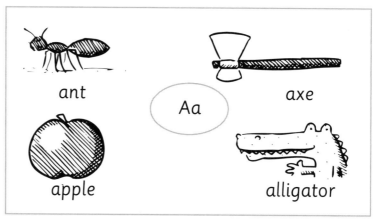

ant · axe · apple · alligator · Aa

FIGURE 1

Using large wooden templates of lower case letters, draw around each letter of the alphabet onto paper. Photocopy these onto A4-size card so that children can stick pictures of objects onto them. Ideally, these need to be cut out for use in the class Big Book.

Make individual alphabet books (one for each child) in the small unlined exercise books, writing a letter of the alphabet on each page in upper and lower case.

Make letter charts (see Figure 2 below).

Aa · Bb · Cc

FIGURE 2

### Introduction

Share a large ABC book (preferably a Big Book). Talk about the cover and see if the children know what sort of book it is and what it is likely to contain. Look through some of the pages talking about the letters and giving them their names, then looking at the pictures on the page and the sound the letter makes for that word. You may wish to explain to the children that sometimes sounds are represented by different letters (as in 'giant' and 'jam', 'camel' and 'kangaroo', 'ceiling' and 'sun', 'fun' and 'potato') if this arises from the discussion.

### Whole-class skills work

Using a large sheet of paper on a flip chart, choose a letter to write in the middle of the page. Write both upper and lower case versions and explain it is the same letter, the capital letter is just used to show something important, such as their names. Now show the children a number of objects in a bag or box (all beginning with the same letter). Write the names of the objects around the letters on the page, including some quick sketches, if you wish. Explain to the children that this will form a page for the class ABC Big Book.

### Differentiated group activities

1: Working from large cut-out letters photocopied onto card, children cut out (or select already cut out) pictures of objects beginning with the same letter. Pictures from magazines could be used for this, or the bank of pictures from photocopiable pages 52–54.

2*: Shared writing with the teacher of words beginning with the chosen letter. Use the objects displayed earlier or, alternatively, choose a different letter and find pictures of objects that begin with that. Children could draw or paint some of the different objects, which can then be stuck to the page. This will form a page for the class ABC Big Book.

3: Pairs use the computer and an alphabet program, while others use the alphabet box (containing a selection of games, jigsaws, mounted alphabet cards with picture clues and a range of alphabet books).

### Conclusion

Ask a few children to show their cut-out letters with pictures and examples of drawings and corresponding words. Sing an alphabet song, possibly to the tune of 'Twinkle, Twinkle, Little Star'.

### Introduction

Engage the children in shared reading of further examples of ABC books (possibly themed versions such as *Alfie's Alphabet* by Shirley Hughes (or *A is for Africa* or *I is for India*, published by Frances Lincoln and slightly more sophisticated, but beautiful photographic books). Then work with the class to write collaboratively a further page for the class ABC Big Book.

### Whole-class skills work

Play 'I Spy'. Write the words 'I spy with my little eye something beginning with ...' on the flip chart, then add the word when a child guesses it. Allow several children to have a turn.

### Differentiated group activities

1*: Shared writing with the teacher of words beginning with the same letter (as Group 2 in Hour 1, but choose a different letter). Children should draw objects and write their own words to match.

2: Pairs use the computer and an alphabet program, while others work from the alphabet box (select which of the games, jigsaws, mounted alphabet cards with picture clues and alphabet books are most suitable for this ability group).

3: Listen to alphabet songs on tape with alphabet books.

### Conclusion

A few children could show examples of their work. Play 'I spy' to finish, using both letter names and sounds. Give extra clues to those who find it difficult, perhaps 'I spy with my little eye something beginning with the letter 'c' making the sound 'k' and it is on the wall and has numbers on it'.

### Introduction

Engage the children in shared reading of more examples of ABC books, including the class ABC Big Book. Write another page of the class ABC Big Book as in Hour 2.

### Whole-class skills work

Make a washing line of letters of the alphabet by attaching with strong thread, or pegs, the upper case letters to the line with the lower case versions hanging underneath (see illustration below). Ask the children to help you decide where each letter should go, referring to a classroom frieze to help. Talk about the capital and lower case letters being different versions of the same letters and ask the children where else they have seen capital letters (they may mention company names such as BBC, B & Q, C & A and MFI, as well as the letters on the computer keyboard).

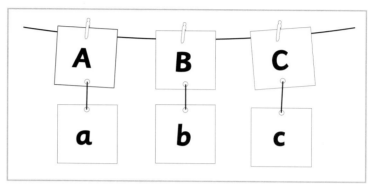

### Differentiated group activities

1: Make individual ABC books in the unlined exercise books into which you have already written an upper and lower case version of each letter of the alphabet. Children should draw pictures for each letter, adding the words if they know them or can find them in dictionaries or the class word bank.

2: Working with large cut-out letters, children cut out pictures of objects beginning with a chosen letter (as for Group 1 in Hour 1). Provide a limited selection of pictures from photocopiable pages 52–54.

3*: Look at a selection of objects beginning with the chosen letter. Model writing the words onto large sheets of paper to go into the class ABC Big Book. Look at simple picture dictionaries to reinforce this. The children then draw pictures, which are later cut out and added to the class ABC Big Book.

### Conclusion

Further pages for the class ABC Big Book should be shown, as well as examples of individual books. Finish by singing an alphabet song, pointing at the letters on the washing line at the same time.

### Introduction

Engage the children in shared reading of the class ABC Big Book. Sing an alphabet song to reinforce alphabetical order, pointing to the letters at the same time.

### Whole-class skills work

Write some words on large card and ask selected children to decide where they could go in the class ABC Big Book. Do the same with pictures of objects and some of the pupils' names. These could be clipped temporarily to the relevant pages.

Using cards with the letters of the alphabet written or printed on, demonstrate to the children how to put cards in the correct place in a card index box.

### Differentiated group activities

1*: Make an ABC index box. Write the letters (upper and lower case) on each card, talking with the children as you do so. Starting with the letter 'a' ask the children for some words that begin with the letter (look at simple picture dictionaries to help with this). Write their suggested words in place and, when you have written a few words on each card (leaving space next to each word for a picture to be drawn), give each child a card so that he or she can draw in some pictures and add any other words and pictures found in dictionaries.

2: Make individual ABC books from the unlined exercise books into which you have already written an upper and lower case letter for each letter of the alphabet. Children should draw pictures for the letters and practise letter formation.

3: Children play 'Hunt the letter'. They should cut out examples of letters from a variety of sources, such as newspapers or magazines, to stick onto the letter charts (see Figure 2 on page 48).

### Conclusion

Group 1 children should show examples of their cards and where they fit in the card index box. Children from Group 3 might show examples of charts of letters and discuss the differences in typeface, size of letters, and use of capitals or lower case. Finish by asking the children to sit in a circle and, using large wooden letters, make an alphabet sun (putting the letters into alphabetical order in a circle). Encourage different children to help.

## HOUR 5

### Introduction and whole-class skills work

Using a laminated version of an ABC book (this could be the already-completed pages of the class version), or acetate sheets clipped to a Big Book, read a page, or a few pages, and then explain that you are looking for capital letters. Demonstrate by circling one, using a non-permanent marker pen. Now choose different children to find a capital letter and put a ring around it.

### Differentiated group activities

1: As for Group 3 in Hour 4. Using A4 charts, stick on examples of letters from magazines and papers. Extend this by including more letters on the page.

2*: As for Group 1 in Hour 4. Continue with making cards for the card index box. The children should add pictures for words you have written and look for more examples in simple dictionaries.

3: Work on individual ABC books, drawing pictures for each letter. The words can be scribed by the teacher later.

### Conclusion

 Show examples of individual ABC books and charts. Remind the children of the capital letters that they found in the Big Book. Ask them to sit in a circle and play a game of 'Snap' with lower and upper case letters, taking turns to turn over the cards.

Alphabet
Picture
Cards

# ALPHABET PICTURES: 2

# ALPHABET PICTURES: 3

# THE GINGERBREAD MAN (1)

## OBJECTIVES

| UNIT | SPELLING/VOCABULARY | GRAMMAR/PUNCTUATION | COMPREHENSION/ COMPOSITION |
|---|---|---|---|
| READING FICTION AND POETRY Traditional tales. | Learn key words using cloze, tracking and posting games. | Know that words are ordered left to right and need to be read that way to make sense. | Recognize storybook language. Be able to locate and read parts of a text. Fit parts of a story into a structure. |

## ORGANIZATION (5 HOURS)

| INTRODUCTION | WHOLE-CLASS SKILLS WORK | DIFFERENTIATED GROUP ACTIVITIES | CONCLUSION |
|---|---|---|---|
| **HOUR 1** Shared reading of story using Big Book. Join in with refrain. Reinforce one-to-one matching using a pointer. | Identify key words 'you', 'and', 'he' in the text with a masking card. Match words printed on card to words in text. | 1*: Guided reading of text/listen to story on tape with half the group while others learn the refrain (exchange). 2: Post key words and track them in the text. 3: Retell story using storyboard. | Selected pupils show key words in text. Group 3 children retell story orally, modelling storybook language and using storyboard. |
| **HOUR 2** Shared reading of text emphasizing the refrain by underlining. Model a 'story map'. Write characters' names on story map. | Look at rhyming words. | 1: Retell the story with the storyboard, recording on tape. 2*: Guided reading, identifying rhyming words with half the group while others draw story maps (exchange). 3: Post key words and track them in the text. | Selected pupils retell the story using story maps. Listen to pupils' tape of story. |
| **HOUR 3** Shared reading of the story identifying the beginning, middle and end of the story. | Fix names of characters next to pictures on the storyboard. Selected children try to match words and pictures. | 1: Draw pictures for the beginning, middle and end of story. 2: Retell and tape the story using the storyboard. 3*: Guided reading of story with half the group while others draw own story maps (exchange). | Group 1 pupils show beginning, middle and end of the story. Display as a 'wall story'. Listen to Group 2's version of the story. |
| **HOUR 4** Shared reading of different versions of the story of the Gingerbread Man. Look at differences, particularly in the characters. | Write speech bubbles to go with figures from the storyboard. Read with the class. | 1*: Guided reading of different versions of the story with half the group while others do a cloze exercise of the refrain (exchange). 2: Track key words in text. Write sentences. 3: Draw characters. | Selected pupils discuss different versions of the story. Group 1 children show cloze exercise – the rest of the class check that it is correct. |
| **HOUR 5** Re-enact the story with pupils taking different parts and the whole class joining in with the refrain. | Pupils hold up the refrain on card for the class to read at appropriate moments. | 1: Draw a picture of each character and write the name. 2*: Guided reading of versions of the story with half the group while others complete cloze (exchange). 3: Listen to class taped versions of the story. | Selected pupils talk about different versions of the story. |

## RESOURCES

Different versions of the story of The Gingerbread Man (including a Big Book version – see main Introduction, page 10 on making your own), audio tape of the story (such as the Ladybird book and tape set, ISBN 0-7214-4955-7), photocopiable pages 59 and 60 (The Gingerbread Man), 61 (Gingerbread Man Characters) and 62 (Run, Run As Fast As You Can!), tape recorder/listening centre and headphones, storyboard, posting boxes, key words ('you', 'and', 'the') on card, laminated card speech bubbles, a board or flip chart, A3 paper, card, Blu-Tack, writing materials.

## PREPARATION

Make an enlarged photocopy of the story from photocopiable pages 59 and 60 plus enough copies of these sheets, and photocopiable page 61, for the whole class. Make enough copies of photocopiable page 62 for Groups 1 and 2. If you do not already have a storyboard you can make one by covering a large wooden board with felt, then make characters for it by colouring and mounting onto card the figures from photocopiable page 61. Attach a small piece of Velcro to each one. Alternatively, if the characters are cut out in felt they will stick directly onto the felt board.

Make six sets of key words on card (you, and, he) and prepare three posting boxes by cutting out a slot from three small boxes and sticking one of the key words on the outside of each one. (If you cover the boxes with sticky-backed plastic then you will be able to peel the word off and replace it with another without damaging the box.)

Divide A3 paper into three equal sections, entitled 'The Gingerbread Man' ruling a line roughly 6cm from the bottom of the page.

Make speech bubbles by cutting out some shaped pieces of card and laminating these. Print out the refrain from the story in large print, leaving out a few words. Write out the missing words on separate cards so that the children can fix them on with small blobs of Blu-Tack.

### HOUR 1

### Introduction

Read the story of the Gingerbread Man, using either the copy which you have enlarged or a Big Book version of the story. Use a pointer to reinforce the matching of one spoken word to one written word, and the direction of print. Encourage the children to join in with the refrain 'Run, run as fast as you can…'.

Ask the children questions about the characters in the story, such as 'What was the Gingerbread Man like?' 'Do they think he should have said no-one could catch him?' You may like to give them some examples of the types of boasting they may have experienced in the playground.

Ask the children if they know any other stories that begin with 'Once upon a time…'.

### Whole-class skills work

Show the key words 'you', 'and', 'he' on card and explain that you are going to look for these words in the story. Highlight one example by using the masking card (see main Introduction, page 12) and then read the surrounding sentence. Choose different children to find other examples.

### Differentiated group activities

1*: Guided reading of the text with half the group, using photocopies of the story. Give each child a copy and ask them to point to the words as you are reading. Encourage them to join in with the reading, particularly with the refrain. Meanwhile the rest of the group listen to the taped version of the story using copies of the text (if it is a commercial tape and book set) or photocopies of the story. They could practise the refrain with a partner after they have listened to the story. Exchange tasks after about 10 minutes.

2: Post sets of the key words 'you', 'he', 'and' into the correct posting boxes. Children may then underline or highlight the key words in photocopies of the text.

3: Use the storyboard and cut-out characters to retell the story.

### Conclusion

Ask a few children to help with an oral retelling of the story. They should use the storyboard and model storybook language. Group 2 children could also show where they found examples of key words in the text.

### Introduction

Re-read the text, emphasizing the refrain, and underlining it each time you reach it on the enlarged photocopy. Now talk about the journey taken by the Gingerbread Man and draw a story map (see below) adding the characters' names.

### Whole-class skills work

Ask the children if they noticed anything about any of the words in the refrain (they may have spotted that they rhyme – if not, point out the rhyme in 'can' and 'ran').

### Differentiated group activities

1: Cut out the characters from photocopiable page 61 and work in pairs to sequence characters and retell the story. If extra adult help is available, ask the children to retell the story onto tape using the storyboard and characters as a prompt.
2*: Read the text with half the group using photocopies of the story as in Hour 1. Ask the children to point out some of the words which sound the same, or rhyme. The rest of the group draw their own story maps based on the example you showed them in the Introduction. Exchange tasks after about 10 minutes.
3: Post sets of key words 'you', 'he', 'and' into the correct posting boxes. Use photocopies of part of the text to underline or highlight the key words.

### Conclusion

Ask a few children to retell the story using their story maps. Listen to any recordings of the story that have been made and encourage comment on whether anything was missed out and whether storybook language such as 'Once upon a time...' was used.

### Introduction

Remind the children of the story of The Gingerbread Man and, using large sheets of paper on a board or flip chart, divide the paper into three sections. Explain to the class that you are going to draw what happened at the beginning of the story in the first box and ask them to tell you what happened first in the story. (You will need to make clear that it is just the very first part of the story that you are dealing with at this stage.) Some children will find this difficult so, as you draw, talk about what happened first.

Draw the first part of the story (try to include as much detail as you can so that children see you model this and, when they later do their own, will be encouraged to do more than just a quick outline – it doesn't have to be brilliant artwork, just detailed!). Next talk about the end of the story (the concept of middle is quite difficult) and draw the ending, again adding lots of detail. Point out that one section of the page remains blank, and in this should be added the rest of the story. Ask the children to suggest what to put in this space while you draw it. By doing this you will have separated the story into the structure of beginning, middle and end in a clear and manageable way.

### Whole-class skills work

Talk about the characters' names and, either writing onto your story map or using the storyboard, fix the names (on card) next to the characters. Selected children could also be asked to match the names to the characters.

### Differentiated group activities

1: Draw pictures for the beginning, middle and end of the story on A3 paper.
2: Cut out the characters from photocopiable page 61 and work in pairs to sequence the characters and retell the story. If extra adult help is available, ask the children to retell the story onto tape using the storyboard and characters as a prompt.

3*: Guided reading of the text with half the group, using photocopies of the story. Allow the children to have one copy each and encourage them to point to the words as you read, or even join in with the reading. Meanwhile the rest of the group draw their own story maps. Exchange tasks after about 10 minutes.

### Conclusion

A number of children might show their versions of the beginning, middle and end of the story. Examples of these can be used to form a 'wall story' for display. If Group 2 have taped a version of the story, listen to this as a class.

### Introduction

Show the class the assortment of different versions of The Gingerbread Man story. The children may want to bring other copies from home to add to the collection. Talk about traditional stories and how they were often told, rather than written down, and explain that that is why different versions exist. Discuss the characters, and point out that some versions have a different number of characters. Talk about how these characters differ.

### Whole-class skills work

Set up the figures on the storyboard and add speech bubbles, using the prepared laminated bubble shapes and writing with a non-permanent pen. Ask the children to suggest some of the things the characters might say in the story.

### Differentiated group activities

1*: Guided reading of a different version of the story with half the group. If possible give each child a copy of the text or, if you only have one copy, try to display it so that everyone can see the print. The rest of the group complete a group cloze exercise of the refrain on photocopiable page 62. Exchange tasks after about 10 minutes.
2: Underline or highlight the key words 'you', 'the' 'and' on photocopies of the text (photocopiable pages 59 and 60). Then write a sentence which uses each word.
3: Draw pictures of characters in the story. Allow the children to choose which ones.

### Conclusion

Ask a few children to talk about different versions of the story that they have read. Group 2 children show their completed cloze and the rest of the class check that it is correct.

### Introduction and whole-class skills work

Explain to the class that they are going to act out the story of The Gingerbread Man. Choose children to take the various parts (you will need to decide in advance which characters to include, although it is probably a good idea to have as many as possible). Now choose two more children to hold up the refrain printed onto card (the one used in the cloze exercise would be useful for this).

First practise the refrain, with one child holding up the card with the words and another using a pointer to point to the words as everybody reads them. Then ask the class to sit in a semi-circle, with the main characters at the front. It may be possible to include the performance in an assembly, or invite parents to come and watch.

### Differentiated group activities

1: Draw a picture of each character in the story and write the character's name underneath. (This will be made easier if you write the characters' names on a list, or on the board, so the group can see it.)
2*: Guided reading of a different version of the story with half the group while the others complete the cloze exercise of the refrain on photocopiable page 62 as in Hour 4. Exchange tasks after about 10 minutes.
3: Listen to commercially-recorded or class versions of the story on tape.

### Conclusion

Select a few children to talk about different versions of the story and the different characters in them. Leave some of their own story tapes available by the listening centre so that the children can listen to them again later.

# THE GINGERBREAD MAN

Once upon a time there lived an old woman and an old man in a little house on a farm.

One day, the old woman was baking some gingerbread. She made the dough and rolled it out. Then she cut it into the shape of a man. She counted out some currants for his eyes, nose, mouth and buttons. Finally, she put the Gingerbread Man on a tray and put it in the oven. Just as she closed the oven, she was sure the Gingerbread Man winked at her. Later, when it was cooked, she opened the oven door and, to her surprise, the Gingerbread Man jumped off the tray and out of the oven, shouting:

"Run, run as fast as you can,
You can't catch me, I'm the Gingerbread Man!"

The woman's husband, who was working in the fields, shouted to the Gingerbread Man: "Stop! Stop!" but the Gingerbread Man kept on running and shouted back:

"Run, run as fast as you can,
You can't catch me, I'm the Gingerbread Man!"

The old woman and the old man ran after the Gingerbread Man as fast as they could. They ran past some children playing, who shouted to the Gingerbread Man: "Stop! Stop!" but the Gingerbread Man kept on running and shouted back:

"Run, run as fast as you can,
You can't catch me, I'm the Gingerbread Man!"

After the Gingerbread Man ran the old woman, the old man and the children and they ran as fast as they could until they ran past their cow called Fran. The cow started to run too and shouted: "Stop! Stop!" but the Gingerbread Man kept on running and shouted back:

"Run, run as fast as you can,
You can't catch me, I'm the Gingerbread Man!"

So, after the Gingerbread Man ran the old woman, the old man, the children and the cow and they kept on running until they ran past a horse eating bran. The horse began to gallop after them, shouting: "Stop! Stop!" but the Gingerbread Man kept on running and shouted back:

"Run, run as fast as you can,
You can't catch me, I'm the Gingerbread Man!"

Now, after the Gingerbread Man ran the old woman, the old man, the children, the cow and the horse and they ran and ran until they passed a dog called Dan. He stopped chewing his bone to shout: "Stop! Stop!" but the Gingerbread Man kept on running and shouted back:

"Run, run as fast as you can,
You can't catch me, I'm the Gingerbread Man!"

So, after the Gingerbread Man ran the old woman, the old man, the children, the cow, the horse and the dog and they ran and ran as fast as they could until they nearly ran into a cat asleep on a van. The cat woke up, and shouted: "Stop! Stop!" but the Gingerbread Man kept on running and shouted back:

"Run, run as fast as you can,
You can't catch me, I'm the Gingerbread Man!"

The Gingerbread Man ran on and on until at last he reached a very deep, wide river. Just then a fox came by.
"Hello," said the fox. "Do you want some help to cross the river? Jump onto my tail. I'll swim across and get you safely to the other side."
The Gingerbread Man wanted to get across quickly before the people who were chasing him got there, so he said, "Thank you" and jumped onto the fox's tail.
The fox swam out into the river with the Gingerbread Man on his tail. Then he said, "You will have to get onto my back. It's getting deeper." So the Gingerbread Man got onto the fox's back.
"It's getting even deeper," said the fox. "You had better get onto my head." The Gingerbread Man climbed onto the fox's head and sat there until the fox said, "It's getting deeper still. Jump onto my nose."
So the Gingerbread Man did and, suddenly, "SNAP!" The fox's mouth opened and he swallowed the Gingerbread Man in one big gulp.
So there was no Gingerbread Man for the old woman, the old man, the cow called Fran, the horse who ate bran, the dog called Dan or the cat who liked to sleep on the van. But the very next day the old woman got out her pan and made another Gingerbread Man.

# GINGERBREAD MAN CHARACTERS

# RUN, RUN AS FAST AS YOU CAN!

■ Fill in the blanks.

Run, _____, as fast as you _____,

_____ can't catch _____,

I'm _____ Gingerbread _____.

# THE GINGERBREAD MAN (2)

## OBJECTIVES

| UNIT | SPELLING/VOCABULARY | GRAMMAR/PUNCTUATION | COMPREHENSION/ COMPOSITION |
|---|---|---|---|
| WRITING FICTION AND POETRY Traditional tales. | Explore rhyming sounds and spelling patterns of rime -an. Identify words beginning with r, m and c. Practise correct letter formation. | Write characters' names using capital letters. | Be able to take part in writing a class version of the story. Make individual books of the characters in the story. |

## ORGANIZATION (5 HOURS)

| | INTRODUCTION | WHOLE-CLASS SKILLS WORK | DIFFERENTIATED GROUP ACTIVITIES | CONCLUSION |
|---|---|---|---|---|
| HOUR 1 | Re-read the story from photocopiable pages 59 and 60. Emphasize the rhyming words. Shared writing of beginning of class story of The Gingerbread Man. | Find words beginning with the consonant r. Demonstrate correct letter formation. | 1: Make individual zigzag books of characters in the story. 2: Write words using initial consonant r. 3*: Shared writing of class story. | Read pages from the class book. Selected pupils show examples of their books and words beginning with r. |
| HOUR 2 | Write a list of the characters in the story. Discuss what they were doing when they saw the Gingerbread Man. | Look at rhyming -an words. Generate words by analogy. | 1: Track words with -an rime in the text. Use magnetic letters to make more words. 2*: Shared writing of class story. 3: Make zigzag books of characters. | Shared reading of page(s) of class book. Selected pupils show their zigzag books and words with -an rime. |
| HOUR 3 | Shared writing of the middle of the story. Refer to previous story maps and wall stories to help. | Find words beginning with the consonant m. Demonstrate correct letter formation. | 1*: Shared writing and reading of further parts of class story. 2: Work on zigzag books. 3.Draw pictures and write words beginning with m. (Groups 1 and 2 exchange.) | Shared reading of middle of story. Selected pupils to show words beginning with m. |
| HOUR 4 | Shared writing of the end of the story. | Look at words beginning with consonant c. Talk about other ways of writing the c sound. Look at words that rhyme with ran. | 1: Complete individual zigzag books. 2*: Shared writing and reading to complete the class story. 3: Match rhyming words pictures. | Selected pupils share their zigzag books. Make up sentences using -an words. |
| HOUR 5 | Shared reading of class book, reinforcing -an words, particularly at the end of the story. | Reinforce making words by analogy from -an. | 1: Use onset and rime dice to make, and list, -an words. 2: Handwriting practice of letters r, m and c. 3*: Complete zigzag books (teacher scribes sentences). | Selected pupils show lists of -an words and examples of handwriting. Play onset and rime dice with the whole class. |

## RESOURCES
Photocopiable pages 59 and 60 (The Gingerbread Man), 67 (Rhyming Word Pictures) and 68 (Onset and Rime Dice), picture dictionaries.

Writing materials, including large (A2) paper and card, A4 and A5 sheets of paper, sugar paper, handwriting books or paper, yellow felt-tipped pen.

A collection of objects to correspond to the pictures on photocopiable page 67, objects that begin with the letters *r*, *m* and *c*, magnetic letters, board or flip chart.

## PREPARATION
Buy a blank Big Book (or make one using A2-size card and paper folded. This can later be bound or stapled together – see main Introduction, page 10 ).

Photocopy, enlarge and laminate The Gingerbread Man story (photocopiable pages 59–60). In addition make enough copies of the story for you and a group to have one each. Photocopy two sets of rhyming word pictures (from photocopiable page 67), laminate these and cut them up.

Prepare onset and rime dice by making a copy of photocopiable page 68, laminating, scoring along the fold lines and sticking the edges together. The joins can be reinforced with adhesive tape.

Make zigzag books by cutting sugar paper slightly larger than A5 paper and folding it to make six pages. (See main Introduction, page 12.)

Make a list of the characters' names in the story.

### Introduction
Begin by reminding the children of the story of The Gingerbread Man from the previous unit. Re-emphasize the use rhyming words and explain that the class is going to write its own version of the story. Write the opening sentences of the story, talking about storybook language.

### Whole-class skills work
Now talk about the refrain 'Run, run as fast as you can...' and circle the letter *r* on the enlarged copy of the story. If you have laminated the pages, use a non-permanent pen and wipe it out afterwards. Talk about the letter *r* and words that begin with it. You could have a selection of objects beginning with *r* to reinforce this. Demonstrate on a board or flip chart the correct letter formation of *r*, while the children 'sky write' the letter at the same time.

### Differentiated group activities
1: Make individual zigzag books of the characters in the story. Give the children a piece of A5-size paper on which to draw a picture of the character and (in a space at the bottom, you can rule a line across to separate it) to write a sentence beginning each time 'I am.....' with the character's name. Emphasize the use of capital letters for the beginnings of names. Provide the group with a list of characters, or write these on the board for them to copy. (The A5 sheets will later need to be mounted onto sugar paper which has been folded to make a zigzag book.)

2: On A4 paper write words beginning with *r* and illustrate them. Provide a selection of picture dictionaries to help with this.

3*: Shared writing of the class story of The Gingerbread Man. Let the children suggest what should be written, and talk about the process as you write it down for them – pointing out such things as the spacing between words and what each word represents.

### Conclusion
Whole-class shared reading of the beginning of the class story of The Gingerbread Man started by Group 3. Some children should show their own books of characters, and words and pictures that begin with the letter *r*.

### Introduction
Talk about the characters in the story of The Gingerbread Man. Write a list of the characters, emphasizing the use of capital letters for the beginnings of names, and talk about what the characters were doing when they saw the Gingerbread Man run by.

## Whole-class skills work

Using magnetic letters, show how a word can be changed by using a different initial letter: *ran, man, can, pan, van*. Follow this by looking at the word *ran*, underlining it in the enlarged text.

## Differentiated group activities

1: Track words with the *-an* rime on a photocopy of the story. Use magnetic letters to make further words which use the *-an* rime.
2*: Shared writing of the class story of The Gingerbread Man (as Group 3 in Hour 1).
3: Make individual zigzag books of the characters in the story (as Group 1 in Hour 1).

## Conclusion

Continue shared reading of the class version of the story. Select children to show examples of their pictures of characters, and words with the *-an* rime highlighted in text. Reinforce this by using magnetic letters to demonstrate a word with the *-an* rime, then making a different word by changing the onset.

## Introduction

Begin by continuing the shared writing of the middle of the story of The Gingerbread Man. You may refer to previous work on story maps and wall stories to help with this.

## Whole-class skills work

Talk about the letter *m* and words that begin with *m*, using objects with this initial sound as reinforcement. Demonstrate the correct letter formation of *m* while the children copy using 'sky writing'.

## Differentiated group activities

1*: Shared writing of further parts of the class story of The Gingerbread Man. Re-read some of the pages with the group.
2: Make individual zigzag books of the characters in the story as in Hours 1 and 2.
3: Draw pictures and write words beginning with the letter *m*. Provide simple picture dictionaries to help, as well as the objects used earlier.

## Conclusion

Shared reading of the middle section of the class story. Ask a few children to show words beginning with the letter *m* and individual zigzag books.

## Introduction

Engage the children in further shared writing of the story of The Gingerbread Man.

## Whole-class skills work

Talk about letters that begin with the letter *c* and show some relevant objects. Point out that the sound *c* can be written in different ways (for example *k* )and that the letter *c* does not always make the same sound (as in the words *cat* and *city*). Model correct letter formation, and select a few children to demonstrate. Now look at words that rhyme with *ran* in the story.

## Differentiated group activities

1: Complete individual zigzag books of the characters in the story.
2*: Shared writing to complete the class story.
(Groups 1 and 2 exchange tasks after 10 minutes.)
3: Match rhyming word pictures (from photocopiable page 67) with the corresponding objects (if available). This might be extended by asking children to pick out the *-an* rhymes and also by having two sets of rhyming pictures and playing a pairs game.

## Conclusion

Allow a few children to share their zigzag books of characters. Show examples of rhyming pictures and objects. Re-read the final paragraph of the photocopiable version of The Gingerbread Man story and make up some further sentences using the *-an* rime. Write these on the board for the class to read.

### Introduction
Read the whole of the class version of the story of The Gingerbread Man encouraging everyone to join in. You may like to ask different children to point to words and show where to begin reading on each page.

### Whole-class skills work
Reinforce the rhyming pattern -an, then, using the enlarged, laminated version of the story, ask the children to help you work through it, underlining examples of words that rhyme with ran.

### Differentiated group activities
1: Use onset and rime dice (made from photocopiable page 68) to create -an words.
2: Practise writing the letters r, m and c. Use handwriting books or paper, with a line of letters already written in yellow felt-tipped pen for the children to overwrite. They can then continue to practise on their own. A box can be drawn on each page for a picture to illustrate that letter.
3*: Complete the zigzag books. The children dictate sentences for the teacher to scribe.

### Conclusion
Selected children show their lists of -an words and examples of handwriting. Play an onset and rime dice game with the whole class – the children take turns to throw both dice and see if they can make a word, if they do, they get a point.

# RHYMING WORD PICTURES

# ONSET AND RIME DICE

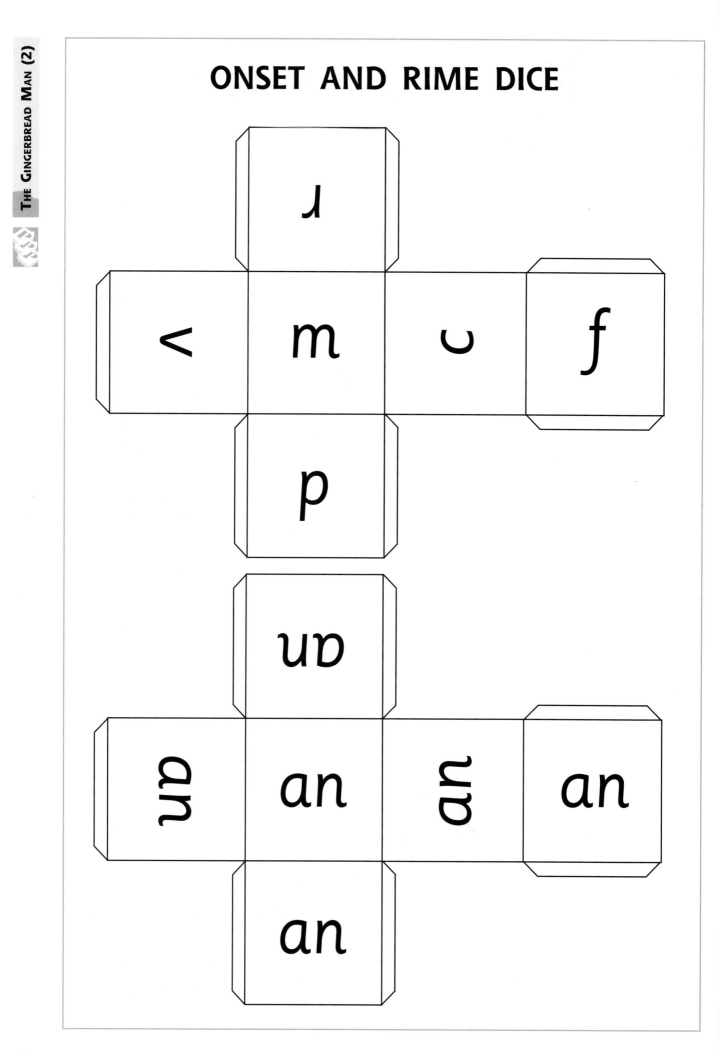

# READING NOTICES AND SIGNS

## OBJECTIVES

| UNIT | SPELLING/VOCABULARY | GRAMMAR/PUNCTUATION | COMPREHENSION/COMPOSITION |
|---|---|---|---|
| READING NON-FICTION Notices and signs (Environmental print). | Use phonic and contextual cues to decipher new words. | Recognize capital letters and their corresponding lower case letters. | Recognize printed and handwritten words in a variety of settings. |

## ORGANIZATION (2 HOURS)

| | INTRODUCTION | WHOLE-CLASS SKILLS WORK | DIFFERENTIATED GROUP ACTIVITIES | CONCLUSION |
|---|---|---|---|---|
| HOUR 1 | Read notices and signs around school. Take photographs to put into class scrapbook. | Mask words on notices, then use contextual cues plus the first letter to decode. | 1*: Guided reading of information books with half the group while others match lower case and capital letters (exchange). 2: Match pictures to signs. Match school signs to correct locations on a plan. 3: Role play in class shop. | Group 1 talk about the information books they have read, showing examples of signs and notices. Group 2 use the plan of the classroom to talk about the placing of signs. Share signs from the class shop. |
| HOUR 2 | Look at a selection of shop signs, carrier bags, advertising flyers, packaging and so on. | Look at the use of capital letters in shop signs. Look for other examples of capital letters and discuss where capital letters are used. | 1: Read and sort advertising material. 2: Role play in class newsagent's shop. 3*: Guided reading of information books, looking at the use of capital letters. Others match upper and lower case plastic letters (exchange). | Selected pupils show examples of capital letters in information books. Group 1 pupils show a selection of advertising for the rest of the class to read. |

## RESOURCES

A number of information books (with some, if possible, about shopping), a non-fiction Big Book, a large plan of the classroom, a range of classroom signs and corresponding pictures, a selection of advertising material, including carrier bags and food packaging, props for the class newsagent's shop (such as magazines and newspapers, greetings cards, wrappers from sweets, chocolate bars, and so on), writing materials, card, Blu-Tack, Post-it notes, alphabet strips, camera and film, upper and lower case plastic letters.

## PREPARATION

Ensure that you have a wide selection of labels and notices around the classroom, then draw or cut out corresponding pictures to match the classroom signs. Make a large plan of the classroom in a simplified format, then display this on a wall, preferably at child height.

Choose a selection of props for the class newsagent's shop, make a sign, and other notices such as 'Open' and 'Closed'. Set up the shop in the home corner. In addition, using large print on card, make a selection of signs for different types of shops ('Chemist', 'Supermarket', 'Toy Shop', 'Sweet Shop' and so on). Make alphabet strips of upper and lower case letters, either handwritten onto card or printed on the computer.

### Introduction

Take a class walk around the school looking for examples of print. Talk about notices and signs and read them with the children. If possible, take photos of the print to use later in a scrapbook. Back in class talk about the signs and look for more examples around the room. Choose different children to 'read a sign'. Talk about the purpose of the signs.

### Whole-class skills work

Now, using an example of a sign (such as 'Only two people in the sand'), mask one word (here it might be 'sand') using either a blob of Blu-Tack or a Post-it note. Ask the children what they think the missing word is. If they find this difficult you can carefully peel away the Blu-Tack to reveal the first letter. If there is a picture clue on the sign, such as a bucket and spade, you can talk about how this makes it easier to read the sign.

### Differentiated group activities

1*: Guided reading, with half the group, of an information Big Book, developing contextual cues by masking words. Demonstrate that when we read non-fiction we do not read the whole text, but choose specific parts. Meanwhile the others match lower case and capital plastic letters. They should also look for examples of capital letters in a selection of non-fiction books. Exchange tasks after about 10 minutes.

2: Give the children a selection of signs, and corresponding pictures which you have drawn (or cut out from magazines) and ask them to match the pictures to the signs. If you duplicate signs on view in the classroom they can use these as a guide. They then attach the signs (using Blu-Tack) onto the correct location on the classroom plan.

3: Role play in the class newsagent's shop using a selection of examples of print.

### Conclusion

Group 1 children can discuss the information book they read, mentioning if they found any examples of signs. Selected children from Group 2 can talk about the classroom plan and the signs they have placed on it. The rest of the class should decide if they are in the right place. Examples of environmental print from the class shop may also be read.

### Introduction

Talk with the children about words that they see when they go for a walk or go shopping. Using a selection of advertising material, ask them to read some of the well-known names. Include carrier bags from local shops, and a whole range of food packaging (you will find that they will all be able to read the names of their favourite restaurants!). Later you can make a scrapbook from some of this material.

### Whole-class skills work

Look for examples of capital letters in advertising, particularly brand names, or shop signs. Talk about when we use capital letters and refer to the corresponding lower case letters. If you have an alphabet frieze in your classroom with lower case and capital letters you can refer to this.

### Differentiated group activities

1: Sort a selection of advertising material into categories by reading the labels. The categories could be the types of shops in which they would be found, such as the newsagent, the chemist, the toy shop and the supermarket. If you have made a sign for each type of shop the children should arrange the advertising material and packaging next to the correct sign.

2: Role play in class newsagent's shop using a selection of examples of print.

3*: Guided reading of a non-fiction Big Book with half the group, looking for examples of capital letters. The rest of the group match lower case and capital plastic letters – provide an alphabet strip showing upper and lower case letters to help. Exchange tasks after about 10 minutes.

### Conclusion

Ask Group 3 children to talk about the book they read and the information they found out. Children from Group 1 can show the different shop signs and types of advertising and packaging they have sorted. The rest of the class can decide if the packaging is in the right 'shop'. Ask the children to look out for capital letters in examples of packaging.

# WRITING NOTICES AND SIGNS

## OBJECTIVES

| UNIT | SPELLING/VOCABULARY | GRAMMAR/PUNCTUATION | COMPREHENSION/ COMPOSITION |
|---|---|---|---|
| WRITING NON-FICTION Notices and signs (Environmental print). | Write key words for use on signs and notices. | Write capital letters for use on signs and notices. | Be able to take part in shared writing of notices and directions. |

## ORGANIZATION (3 HOURS)

| | INTRODUCTION | WHOLE-CLASS SKILLS WORK | DIFFERENTIATED GROUP ACTIVITIES | CONCLUSION |
|---|---|---|---|---|
| HOUR 1 | Shared writing of sentences for class scrapbook of signs around school. | Match key words on card to assorted signs. | 1*: Shared writing of signs. 2: Write sentences beginning 'I like', using a selection of advertising material. 3: Match words and pictures from signs. | Selected pupils read signs they have made and then place them in correct position in the classroom. Pupils from Group 2 read examples of their sentences. |
| HOUR 2 | Shared writing of directions around the classroom. | Emphasize the spacing between words and correct letter formation. | 1: Write shopping lists for newsagent's shop. 2*: Shared writing of directions. 3: Role play in newsagent's shop. | Pupils from Group 2 read out directions and choose classmates to follow them. Read out some examples of shopping lists. Can they find all the items in the class shop? |
| HOUR 3 | Shared writing of examples of notices for class notice-board, such as 'Lunch money on Mondays'. | Letter formation of capital letters. | 1: Role play in newsagent's shop 2: Write shopping lists for newsagent's shop. 3*: Shared writing of notices. | Selected pupils read out notices they have written and pin them on the class notice-board. |

## RESOURCES

Photographs taken of notices and signs around the school during Hour 1 of the previous unit (see page 70), selected key words on card (taken from List 1 of the National Literacy Strategy), appropriate pictures for matching with classroom signs (see photocopiable page 74).

A selection of items for use in the class newsagent's shop, such as newspapers, magazines, greetings cards and sweet wrappers.

Writing materials including a yellow felt-tipped pen, A5-size paper for shopping lists, large A3 scrapbook, or large sheets of card folded to make a scrapbook.

Class notice-board with a few notices on it (a section of a wall display area with the heading 'Notice-board' will suffice, but keep this as low as possible so that the children can pin up and read notices), alphabet frieze, board or flip chart, computer (optional).

## PREPARATION

Ensure that you have plenty of examples of environmental print around the classroom. Make cards for key words. Make enough copies of photocopiable page 74 for Group 3.

Make the home corner into a class newsagent's shop (see previous unit, page 69). Prepare a class notice-board.

### Introduction

Remind the class about the walk they took around school to look at notices and signs. Now show them the photographs that were taken. Talk about what these signs were for and write a sentence for one or two of the signs which can be placed under the photograph when it is stuck in a scrapbook. As you write each sentence you can talk about individual words and remind them of the spacing between words as well as the correct letter formation.

### Whole-class skills work

Show the children some examples of key words from List 1 of the National Literacy Strategy for developing sight vocabulary (for example, 'look', 'is', 'play', 'go') and ask if anyone can find the same word around the classroom on a sign or notice. Ask the child to go to the sign and hold the key word next to the appropriate place. Then ask the rest of the class if anyone can read the sign.

If you have some examples of signs that show pictures as well as words, talk about whether this makes them easier to read. Read as many key words in the context of a sentence as you can.

### Differentiated group activities

1*: Discuss signs around the classroom and ask the children to suggest further examples. Write one sign with the children and then ask them to draw a picture for other signs. Ask any children who are able to write appropriate words for the sign, support those who need help by writing on the board for them to copy.
2: Choose an item from a selection of advertising material, such as packaging, then write sentences which begin 'I like ...', followed by the name of the chosen item. Draw a picture of the item underneath.
3*: Using photocopiable page 74, match the signs to the pictures. This could first be done physically by finding the correct sign in the classroom and matching it to the correct picture on the photocopiable sheet.

### Conclusion

Group 1 children show signs they have made and ask the rest of the class to try to read them. Group 2 children show examples of sentences they have written with their chosen items. Talk about examples of print in the newsagent's shop and read some to and with the children.

### Introduction

Talk about directions that you give people to help them find places. Choose individual children to demonstrate this, directing them to a certain area in the classroom. If you blindfold the child (but ask another child to hold his or her hand to avoid bumping into objects), this will emphasize the importance of precise directions and of listening and carrying them out.

### Whole-class skills work

Now explain that you are going to write down some directions. Choose a brief but precise example, such as how to get from the classroom to the school office or the hall. Talk about the writing as you do it, reinforcing the spelling and word recognition of key words, the spacing between words and correct letter formation.

### Differentiated group activities

1: Write a shopping list for use in the class newsagent's shop. Emphasize that they should only include items that can be bought at a newsagent's. They can draw a picture and try to write the word.
2*: Talk about further examples of directions and ask the children to devise directions which you scribe (or key into the computer). Choose a pupil to carry out the directions, so the group will see if they were precise enough, or need to be amended.
3: Role play in the class shop, taking turns to be the shopkeeper and the customers.

## Conclusion

Ask children from Group 2 to read examples of directions and choose classmates to carry them out. Group 1 children can read out their shopping lists and ask the rest of the class decide if the items can be bought in the newsagent's shop.

**HOUR 3**

## Introduction

Have one or two ready-made notices pinned on the class notice-board, perhaps 'Merit assembly on Fridays' or 'Lunch money on Mondays'. Talk about these notices and read them to the class, then discuss why we have notices. Now write a notice to put on the notice-board. Ask the children to suggest something that they need to remember.

## Whole-class skills work

Talk about examples of capital letters in notices and ask different children to point some out. Reinforce the correspondence between capital letters and lower case using the classroom alphabet frieze, or other examples on displays. (You may have capital letters cut out in stiff card and hung along a washing line with the corresponding lower case letter hanging below each one, as suggested in the 'Alphabet Books' unit, Hour 3, page 50.) Now choose one or two capital letters and demonstrate the correct letter formation. Ask the children to 'sky write' the letter and choose one or two to demonstrate on the board or flip chart.

## Differentiated group activities

1: Role play in the class newsagent's shop, taking turns to be the shopkeeper and the customers and making use of environmental print, for example by ensuring that the open and closed signs are appropriately displayed.
2: Write a shopping list for use in the class newsagent's shop, drawing a picture and writing the word, if possible. Provide a list of words, either on paper or on the board, to help with this.
3*: Talk about notices for the class notice-board and ask the children to think of a notice they would like to put on the board. Scribe a notice for each child. (If you do this in yellow felt-tipped pen, marking the starting point for each letter, they can trace over your writing.)

## Conclusion

Ask a few Group 3 children to read notices they have written and pin them on the class notice-board. Examples of completed shopping lists can also be shown, and one or two might be pinned on the class notice-board. Remind the children of signs, notices and directions they have written and ask them to look for examples when they are going for walks. Leave the class scrapbook (see Introduction – Hour 1) of signs in the class book corner so the children can read it later.

# SIGNS AROUND THE CLASSROOM

Writing Area
Please put things away.

Only two children to
play in the sand.

Wash your paint
brushes here.

Put your books away
carefully.

# Term 2

# DEAR ZOO

## OBJECTIVES

| UNIT | SPELLING/VOCABULARY | GRAMMAR/PUNCTUATION | COMPREHENSION/COMPOSITION |
|---|---|---|---|
| READING FICTION AND POETRY *Dear Zoo* by Rod Campbell. 'We've got a Wa Wa' by Rony Robinson. | Read key words in context. Develop phonological awareness through use of alliteration. Recognize rhyming words. | Match suitable adjectives to animals. | Read texts with a predictable structure and patterned language. Relate ideas in text to own experience. Understand and use correctly terms about books and print. |

## ORGANIZATION (5 HOURS)

| | INTRODUCTION | WHOLE-CLASS SKILLS WORK | DIFFERENTIATED GROUP ACTIVITIES | CONCLUSION |
|---|---|---|---|---|
| HOUR 1 | Read *Dear Zoo*. Talk about different pets and the author's ideal pet. | Re-read the book, asking the children to join in. Identify and underline repeated phrases. | 1*: Guided reading of *Dear Zoo* with half the group. Others find ideal pet in animal books (exchange). 2: Make own *Dear Zoo* books. 3: Match animal words and pictures. | Pupils show examples of their own books and ideal pets. Write sentences for different animals for the whole class to read. |
| HOUR 2 | Re-read *Dear Zoo* with the children joining in. Suggest alternative animals and write appropriate sentences for the children to read. | Show key words on card (was, I, me, him) and ask selected pupils to find words in the story. Read surrounding sentence each time. | 1: Track key words in magazines and newspapers. Write a sentence containing the key word. 2*: Guided reading of *Dear Zoo* with half the group. Others find ideal pet in animal books (exchange). 3: Make own *Dear Zoo* books. | Selected pupils show examples of sentences containing key words. Show examples of ideal pets and write suitable sentences for the whole class to read. |
| HOUR 3 | Re-read *Dear Zoo* with key words masked for pupils to guess from context. | Use sentences from the text written on card to match with the text. | 1: Make own *Dear Zoo* books. 2: Track key words using extracts from magazines and newspapers. 3*: Guided reading of *Dear Zoo* with half the group. Others find ideal pet in animal books (exchange). | Selected pupils show examples of their individual books and ideal pets. Re-read a sentence from the text with a key word masked. |
| HOUR 4 | Read enlarged version of poem 'We've got a Wa Wa' on photocopiable pages 80 and 81. | Use examples of alphabet books to demonstrate making an alphabet book. Start a class alphabet frieze. | 1*: Guided reading from a non-fiction book about animals with half the group. Others look at different alphabet books (exchange). 2: Make own animal alphabets. 3: Match animal names to pictures and models. | Selected pupils show examples of their animal alphabets. Were there any letters that they could not find animals for? Match names of animals to pictures and models. Add to class frieze. |
| HOUR 5 | Read an animal alphabet book, either home-made or a published version. | Discuss words to describe the animals. Ask the children to think of words to describe animals on the alphabet frieze which begin with the same sound. | 1*: Write shared sentences to re-read for the class frieze. 2: Match animal names to pictures and models. 3: Make own animal alphabets. | Selected pupils show examples of their animal alphabets. Shared reading of examples of sentences for class frieze. |

## RESOURCES

*Dear Zoo* by Rod Campbell (Picture Puffin, ISBN 0-14-050446-X) – ideally at least six copies – examples of alphabet books (including an animal alphabet book), a number of non-fiction books about animals, simple picture dictionaries.

Photocopiable pages 80 and 81 ('We've got a Wa Wa' by Rony Robinson) and 82–84 (Animal Alphabet Pictures), cards with key words (such as: was, I, me, him) from List 1 of the National Literacy Strategy.

Writing materials, including A5 and A3 white paper, long strips of sugar paper, Blu-Tack, Post-it notes, non-permanent marker pen, drawing materials, board or flip chart.

Extracts from magazines and newspapers for tracking key words (for Groups 1 and 2), a collection of animal pictures from magazines and/or a selection of model animals with corresponding word cards to match, a roll of frieze paper (possibly the blank side of a wallpaper border).

## PREPARATION

Make your own Big Book version of *Dear Zoo* (see main Introduction, page 10). Type the repeated phrases in large type (48 point) onto the computer and print them out ('He was too ......... I sent him back.'), or write them onto card and laminate. Prepare an enlarged, laminated version of the text.

Make a set of key words on card. Prepare zigzag books by folding strips of sugar paper to make six pages in total (see main Introduction, page 12). Write animal words on card to match the picture and/or model collection.

Photocopy and enlarge one copy of the poem 'We've got a Wa Wa' (photocopiable pages 80 and 81). Make enough copies of photocopiable pages 82–84 for Groups 2 and 3.

## SYNOPSIS

This popular lift-the-flap book charts a series of letters that a little boy writes to a zoo asking for a pet. Various animals are rejected until, finally, an ideal pet is found.

### Introduction

Introduce the text of *Dear Zoo* by talking about the cover, title and blurb. Ask the children to predict what the book is about or, if they have read it before, to recall what they can remember about the text.

Read the story, pausing each time for the children to guess what sort of animal is behind the flap. Encourage them to join in with the repeated phrases. When you have finished reading talk about the author's ideal pet and ask the children what their ideal pet would be.

### Whole-class skills work

Re-read the story and encourage everyone to join in. Talk about the words that are the same on each page. Use an enlarged, laminated extract of the text to underline, in non-permanent marker pen, the repeated phrases each time, pointing out which words are the same and which are different.

### Differentiated group activities

1*: Carry out a guided read of small copies of the text with half of the group, while the rest of the group look at a selection of books on animals to find, and draw, their ideal pet. Exchange tasks after about 10 minutes.

2: Make individual zigzag books of *Dear Zoo* using A5 paper (six pages in total, including a title page) with a line ruled about 3cm from the bottom of the page where the teacher can write 'He was too .........' (big, small, etc.). Alternatively, print this onto the page, leaving a blank for the child to add, with your help, the appropriate word. Ask the children to draw an animal on each page, ending with their ideal pet. These can be later pasted onto the sugar paper strips.

3: Select pictures of animals from a collection taken from magazines and match these to the correct words written on card. Alternatively, the pictures could be stuck onto paper and the correct word written underneath each animal.

### Conclusion

Select a few children to show examples of their own books and ideal pets. Ask for suggestions of appropriate sentences for each animal and write these on the board or flip chart for the children to read.

### Introduction

Re-read the text of *Dear Zoo*, encouraging the children to join in. Emphasize one-to-one matching by pointing at the words on the enlarged extract, as you read. Ask the children to suggest alternative animals and write sentences to fit for the children to read (for example, 'So they sent me a crocodile. He was too snappy! I sent him back.').

### Whole-class skills work

Show the children key words on card (was, I, me, him) and ask if they know what they say. Choose a child to find one of the words on the cards within the text in the book. When a word is found, read the whole sentence and ask the children to read it with you.

### Differentiated group activities

1: Track key words (using the ones on card already displayed) in extracts from magazines or newspapers. Ask the children to underline or highlight the words, then write a sentence using one (or more) of the words.
2*: Guided read of the text (using small copies of the text) with half of the group to find sentences with key words in. The rest of the group look at a selection of books on animals to find their ideal pet. Exchange tasks after about 10 minutes.
3: Make individual zigzag books of *Dear Zoo* as Group 2 in Hour 1.

### Conclusion

Select a few children to show examples of sentences with key words in. Some Group 2 children might also show examples of pictures of ideal pets. Finish with some shared writing of suitable sentences for the pets which the whole class can read.

### Introduction and whole-class skills work

Re-read the enlarged version of the text with the key words masked with Post-it notes or Blu-Tack. Pause at the masked words and ask the children to suggest what fits. If they find this difficult gradually reveal the beginning of the word, talking about the sound that letter makes. Show the individual sentences from the text on card and choose different children to match each sentence to the complete story, before reading it.

### Differentiated group activities

1: Make individual zigzag books of *Dear Zoo* as Group 2 in Hour 1.
2: Track key words (using the ones on card already displayed) in extracts from magazines or newspapers underlining or highlighting the words.
3*: Guided read of the text (using small copies of the text) with half of the group to find sentences with key words in. The rest of the group look at a selection of books on animals to find their ideal pet. Exchange tasks after about 10 minutes.

### Conclusion

Ask a few children to show examples of their individual books and their ideal pets. Re-read sentences from the text with a key word masked.

### Introduction

Begin by introducing the enlarged version of the poem 'We've got a Wa Wa'. Ask the children to predict what the poem might be about, possibly looking at the picture that accompanies the poem in *A Very First Poetry Book*, compiled by John Foster (Oxford University Press, ISBN 0-19-916050-3).

Read the poem, emphasizing the rhyme and alliteration. Then talk about the humour and the poet's choice of words. The poem also provides an ideal opportunity to emphasize onset and rime, as in 'runny and funny', 'nobbly and wobbly', 'lumpy and bumpy', 'squelchy and belchy', 'floppy and soppy'.

## Whole-class skills work

Now show examples of alphabet books and talk about making an animal alphabet using the Wa Wa as an animal for w. Ask the children for some other examples of animals. Using the frieze paper, marked in sections for the different letters of the alphabet, write in some of the children's suggestions for different letters. For letters that are difficult to match to suitable animals, encourage the children to make up imaginary animals or pets like the Wa Wa.

## Differentiated group activities

1*: Guided read, with half of the group, of a selected section from a non-fiction book about animals. Talk about the difference between fiction (story books) and non-fiction (information books). Explain that you only need to read a limited part of a non-fiction book and that much of the information can be gained from looking carefully at the pictures or photographs. Meanwhile the rest of the group look at a range of different alphabet books. Exchange tasks after about 10 minutes.
2: Make individual animal alphabets, similar to photocopiable page 82–84, using A3 paper divided into sections for each letter of the alphabet. Ask the children to draw a picture for as many letters as they can, providing simple picture dictionaries to help. If certain letters prove difficult, they could use some of the ideas from photocopiable pages 82–84 (Animal Alphabet Pictures).
3: Match animal names to pictures and/or models.

## Conclusion

Selected children show examples of their animal alphabets. Were there any letters that they could not find animals for? Show the names of animals matched to pictures or models, then ask the children for more examples of animals to write on the class frieze (these could have been found in non-fiction books during the guided reading session).

## Introduction and whole-class skills work

Read an animal alphabet book and discuss the sounds that each animal name begins with. Now discuss words to describe animals. Refer back to the enlarged version of 'We've got a Wa Wa' and look at some of the adjectives used in this. Ask the children to think of words to describe animals on the alphabet frieze which begin with the same sound (amazing alligator, beautiful baboon, clever cat, dirty dog, and so on).

## Differentiated group activities

1*: Work collaboratively to write sentences about animals for the class frieze. These could be non-fiction sentences, or fiction sentences, perhaps containing alliterative adjectives. The sentences could be written on the computer to print out and stick to the frieze.
2: Match animal names to pictures and/or models.
3: Make their own animal alphabet on A3 paper as Group 2 in Hour 4.

## Conclusion

Encourage a few children from Group 3 to show examples of their animal alphabets. Ask Group 1 to read examples of their sentences for the class frieze.

# WE'VE GOT A WA WA

We've got a Wa Wa in our house

Squelchy as an octopus and scratchy as a mouse

Slippy and slurpy

Ever-so dirty

Wet and slimy

And its eyes – cor blimey!

Nose all runny

Cheeks all funny

Claws all queer

And its tail – oh dear!

We've got a Wa Wa comes at night

Waits in my bedroom to give my dad a fright.


We've got a Wa Wa only I can see

Comes out at night but just for me

Nasty and nobbly

Wibbly and wobbly

Sloshy and slow

And its teeth – oh no!

Lips all lumpy

Bum all bumpy

Ears all runny

And its horns – oh mummy!

We've got a Wa Wa, come and see,

Scares my dad, but is very nice to me.

I'm going to bring my Wa Wa to school,

Even if pets are against the rule.

Squiggly and squelchy

Bubbly and belchy

Doesn't wash

And its roar – oh gosh!

Legs all floppy

Feet all soppy

Name you'll find out

Be careful – mind out!

I've got a Wa Wa, pleased to meet you,

If you're nasty, my Wa Wa'll eat you!

*Rony Robinson*

# ANIMAL ALPHABET PICTURES

## ALPHABET PICTURE CARDS

# ANIMAL ALPHABET PICTURES 2

# ANIMAL ALPHABET PICTURES 3

# DEAR FARM

## OBJECTIVES

| UNIT | SPELLING/VOCABULARY | GRAMMAR/ PUNCTUATION | COMPREHENSION/ COMPOSITION |
|---|---|---|---|
| WRITING FICTION AND POETRY Stories with predictable structures and patterned language. | Collect words for word bank. Learn spellings of key words. Identify and write initial/ final phonemes in CVC words. | Use capital letters and full stops to demarcate sentences. | Shared writing of a class book entitled 'Dear Farm'. Emergent writing of letters. Make individual flap books. |

## ORGANIZATION (5 HOURS)

| | INTRODUCTION | WHOLE-CLASS SKILLS WORK | DIFFERENTIATED GROUP ACTIVITIES | CONCLUSION |
|---|---|---|---|---|
| HOUR 1 | Shared letter writing for class book entitled 'Dear Farm'. Pupils suggest different farm animals and suitable ways to describe them. Identify initial and final phonemes in CVC words such as *cat* or *rat*. | Collect words (animal names) for class word bank. | 1*: Shared writing of class book with half the group while others look at dictionaries and animal books for other suitable animals and matching words (exchange). 2: Spell key words 'they' and 'was'. 3: Practise handwriting of CVC words and draw pictures. | Selected pupils from Groups 1 and 3 show examples of pictures and handwriting. Group 2 pupils spell words aloud (using letter names). Whole class reads sentences written for class book. |
| HOUR 2 | Examine examples of flap books and read extracts. Discuss design of flaps for book. Continue shared writing for class book 'Dear Farm'. | Emphasize the use of capital letters and full stops. Highlight these by circling capital letters (in one colour) and full stops (in another colour). | 1: Spell key words 'they', 'was' and 'said'. 2: Practise handwriting of CVC words and draw pictures. 3*: Shared writing for class book/find suitable animals and matching words (exchange). | Selected pupils show handwriting examples. Whole-class oral spelling of 'they' and 'was'. Read further sentences for class book. |
| HOUR 3 | Shared reading of class book 'Dear Farm'. Discuss individual flap books. | Discuss different adjectives used to describe animals. Match words on card to text, then put them into the class word bank. | 1: Practise handwriting of CVC words and sentences. 2*: Make individual flap books. 3: Spell key words 'they' and 'was'. | Selected pupils show their individual flap books and read sentences from them. Discuss use of suitable words to describe animals. Whole-class oral spelling of 'they' and 'was'. |
| HOUR 4 | Shared writing of an example letter beginning 'Dear Farmer'. | Spell common words. Identify initial and final phonemes in words. Make spelling choices. | 1: Independent letter writing with a given framework. 2: Work on onset and rime of CVC words. 3*: Make individual flap books. | Selected pupils show flap books and read sentences from them. Group 1 children read some of their letters. Reinforce words made using *-at* rime. |
| HOUR 5 | Read a further example of a flap book such as *Noisy Farm*. Discuss choice of words. | Spell CVC words using letter names. | 1*: Make individual flap books. 2: Letter writing with a given framework. 3: Work on onset and rime of CVC words using clue cards and plastic letters. | Selected pupils read examples of their letters and individual flap books. Read *-at* words. |

## RESOURCES

A selection of flap books (such as *Noisy Farm* by Rod Campbell – Picture Puffin, ISBN 0-14-050293-9), picture dictionaries, non-fiction books on animals, spelling books.

Photocopiable pages 89 (CVC Handwriting Practice) and 90 (Letter to the Farmer), materials for making individual flap books (A3 paper, craft knife or scissors – see main Introduction, page 13), two sets of clue cards with individual -*at* words (cat, rat, hat, mat and so on), along with a picture, on each one.

Board or flip chart, different-coloured pens, A3 paper or card, computer, magnetic or plastic letters, a puppet (optional).

## PREPARATION

Make a flap book for each child (see instructions in main Introduction, page 13). Write out, or print out on the computer, -*at* words, copy to make two sets, illustrate and laminate. Make enough copies of photocopiable page 89 (CVC Handwriting Practice) for the whole class and enough copies of photocopiable page 90 (Letter to the Farmer) for Groups 1 and 2.

## INTRODUCTION

Remind the children of the story *Dear Zoo*. Ask them if they know when you normally write 'Dear .......' (when writing a letter). Explain that you are going to make a class book, called 'Dear Farm', made up of letters that the class write about farm animals, with a perfect pet at the end of the story.

Now, using different coloured pens and the board or flip chart, model writing a letter, asking the children for suggestions of suitable animals. Begin by writing 'Dear Farm' (or Farmer) in one colour, talking as you write about the use of capital letters and spaces between words. Suggest that each letter could begin with 'Please could you send us an animal for a pet.' and write this in a different colour. Then, in yet another colour, write: 'from Class ...'.

Explain that this will form the model for the children's own letters. Talk about the sounds in words, choosing CVC words such as 'cat' and 'rat'. Highlight initial and final phonemes. You might reinforce this by introducing a puppet who can't hear the initial or final sound and asking the children to help the puppet by repeating the sound several times.

### Whole-class skills work

Write down on large pieces of card the names of the farm animals suggested by the children so that they can read, identify, and then add them to the class word bank. If you have on the wall a large word bank with pockets for each letter of the alphabet, this would be a good opportunity for selected children to put the words in the correct places in the word bank.

### Differentiated group activities

1*: Shared writing of letters for the book with half the group. This could be done on the computer, with the children dictating what to say or, alternatively, hand written on A3 paper or card to form part of the book. Remind the children that they need to choose suitable adjectives to describe the animal which also explain why that particular animal has been rejected, for example: 'They sent me a cow. She was too big. They sent me a horse. He was too hungry. They sent me a pig. He was too smelly.' And so on. You could also add follow-up letters, such as: 'Dear Farmer, Thank you for the pig. I am sending him back. He is too smelly. Please can you send me another animal for a pet?'
Meanwhile the rest of the group choose suitable animals for the story using a selection of picture dictionaries and non-fiction books about animals. Exchange tasks after about 10 minutes.
2*: Use spelling books to learn the spelling of key words ('they' and 'was'). Encourage them to learn to 'Look-say-cover-write-check', fold the page and write without copying.
3: Handwriting practice of CVC words (see photocopiable page 89). Trace over the words, starting at the spot marked and following the direction of the arrow. When they have practised each word, they should draw a picture underneath and try to write the words again without copying.

### Conclusion

Ask a few children to show examples of their handwriting and pictures. Group 2 children might spell aloud words (using letter names). Finish with the whole class reading letters which have been written for the class book.

### Introduction

Show the children one or two other flap books and talk about the format of these books. Read an extract of the text and look at what is behind the flaps. Now talk about the class flap book 'Dear Farm'. Look at some examples of letters written during the previous lesson and ask the class for a suggestion for a further letter. Model writing the letter again as in Hour 1.

### Whole-class skills work

Talk about the use of capital letters and full stops as you use them. Show the laminated version of *Dear Zoo* (from the previous unit) and ask some of the children to help you find the capital letters and full stops. Invite individual children to circle the capital letters in one colour, and the full stops in another colour.

### Differentiated group activities

1: Use spelling books to learn the spelling of key words ('they', 'was' and 'said'). Learn to 'Look-say-cover-write-check', then fold the page and write without copying.
2: Handwriting practice of CVC words (see photocopiable page 89). When they have practised each word they should draw a picture underneath, then try to write the words again without copying.
3*: Shared writing of further letters for the book with half the group, as in Hour 1. Meanwhile the rest of the group choose suitable animals for the story using a selection of picture dictionaries and non-fiction books about animals. Exchange tasks after about 10 minutes.

### Conclusion

Ask a few children to show examples of their handwriting. Then get the whole class to spell 'they' and 'was' orally (Group 1 children could also spell 'said'). Finish with a whole-class reading of further sentences from the class book. Place the finished book in the class book corner for re-reading.

### Introduction

Begin with a shared reading of the class book 'Dear Farm'. Refer to other examples of flap books and remind the children of the format.

### Whole-class skills work

Discuss the different adjectives used to describe animals. Select some of the words, write them on card and ask different children to match them to the text. These words can then be added to the class word bank.

### Differentiated group activities

1: Handwriting practice of CVC words – children copy a selection of words which you have written on the board and then write a sentence containing the words.
2*: Make individual flap books. Write key phrases on card, or on the board for the children to copy. (For example: 'They sent me a ….He was too ….')
3: Spell key words 'they' and 'was' using spelling books.

### Conclusion

Select some Group 2 children to show their individual flap books and read sentences from them. Discuss suitable words to describe animals. Finish with a whole-class oral spelling of 'they' and 'was'.

### Introduction and whole-class skills work

Model a further example of a 'Dear Farmer' letter or show the class one of the letters written in Hours 1 or 2. Talk about the sounds of the letters and the spelling choices as you write the words. Draw the children's attention particularly to initial and final phonemes in words by asking them which sound they can hear, and how they think it is spelled, before you write the word.

### Differentiated group activities

1: Write letters independently, but using a writing frame (possibly photocopiable page 90 – Letter to the Farmer).
2: Use magnetic or plastic letters to investigate words with the -at rime. The children then write a list of the words they make.
3*: Make individual flap books. The children suggest different animals and draw pictures under the flaps. Suitable sentences can be dictated and scribed.

### Conclusion

Select a few children to show their individual flap books and read sentences from them. Group 1 children might also read some of their letters. Show some examples of the words made using the -at rime. Emphasize the beginning and end phonemes in these words.

### Introduction and whole-class skills work

Introduce a flap book, such as *Noisy Farm,* and read it expressively for fun. Discuss the choice of words to describe the animals and compare this with the class flap book, which can also be re-read for fun. Look for examples of CVC words in the text and ask the children to spell them aloud, using letter names. Read the sentences surrounding the words with the children.

### Differentiated group activities

1*: Make individual flap books and write suitable sentences to fit. Key words can be displayed as part of the class word bank.
2: Independent letter writing with a given framework (photocopiable page 90).
3: Work on onset and rime of CVC words (such as: cat, hat, rat, mat) using clue cards (cards with one example of a word with the -at rime, together with a picture) and plastic letters. Children might then play a pairs game with the two sets of -at words on card.

### Conclusion

Choose some Group 2 children to read examples of their letters. Read some of the -at words. Finally select a few flap books to be shown and read.

# CVC HANDWRITING PRACTICE

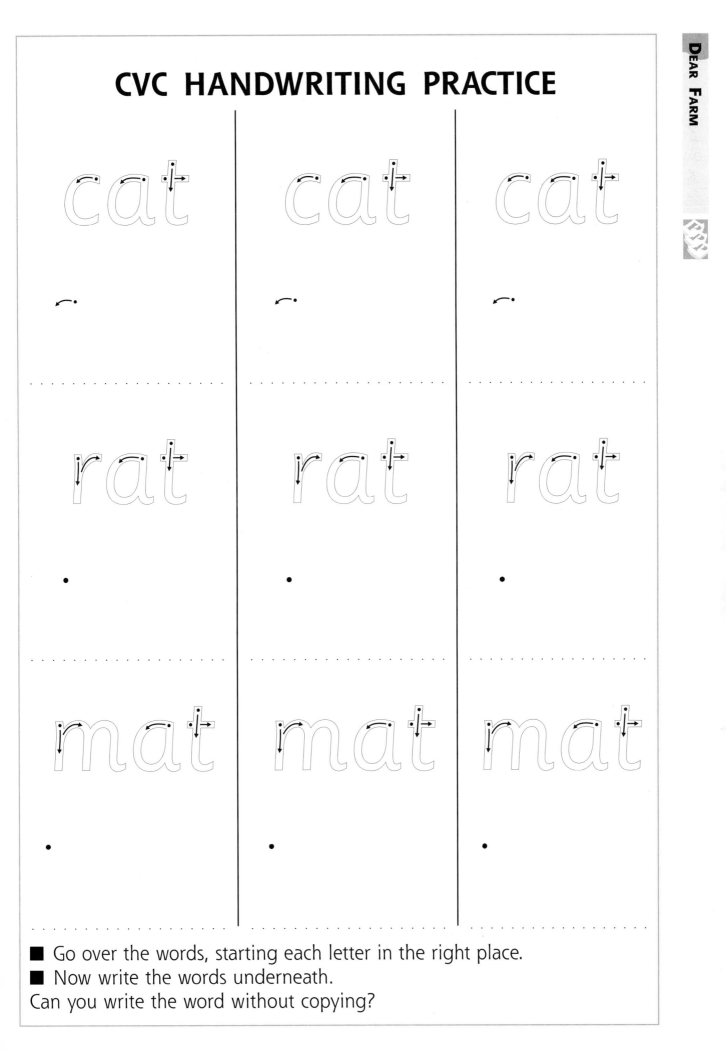

■ Go over the words, starting each letter in the right place.
■ Now write the words underneath.
Can you write the word without copying?

# LETTER TO THE FARMER

_____ School

Dear Farmer,

Please can you send me a _____

Love from _____

# ANIMALS

## OBJECTIVES

| UNIT | SPELLING/VOCABULARY | GRAMMAR/PUNCTUATION | COMPREHENSION/ COMPOSITION |
|---|---|---|---|
| READING NON-FICTION Simple non-fiction texts. | Identify key words. Understand the terms 'photograph', 'illustration' and 'caption'. | Match key words to sentences. Understand that a sentence should make sense. Ask questions and identify question marks. Use capital letter to start a sentence. | Read different non-fiction books on the theme of animals. Distinguish between a photograph and an illustration. Find information from photographs. |

## ORGANIZATION (2 HOURS)

| INTRODUCTION | WHOLE-CLASS SKILLS WORK | DIFFERENTIATED GROUP ACTIVITIES | CONCLUSION |
|---|---|---|---|
| **HOUR 1** Read a non-fiction Big Book on animals. Talk about difference between photographs and illustrations. Look carefully at a photograph and ask or answer questions. | Locate key words in title, contents, index and headings. Make a 'physical sentence' using key words. | 1*: Guided reading with half the group. Others locate books that contain photographs (exchange). 2: Find key words in non-fiction books and write sentences. 3: Use information from photographs to complete photocopiable page. | Selected pupils from Groups 1 and 3 share outcomes of their group work. Pupils re-order mixed-up words to make a sentence that uses key words. |
| **HOUR 2** Look at non-fiction Big Book and remind pupils that photographs give information. Label a photograph and write a suitable caption. | Model writing a sentence using the key words. Pupils read the sentence. | 1: Use information from photographs to complete photocopiable page and write name of animal. 2*: Guided reading with half the group. Others locate books that contain photographs (exchange). 3: Play Kim's game – match words and pictures of animals. | Pupils show photographs located in books and discuss information gained from them. Finish by singing 'Old Macdonald had a farm', with names of animals on card for different children to hold up. |

## RESOURCES

Non-fiction Big Book (ideally, one about animals) containing photographs, selection of non-fiction books, sample illustration to compare with a photograph, animal poster or large photograph, selection of pictures of animals (for example, from magazines).
Photocopiable pages 94 (Animal Information) and 95 (Matching Animal Words and Pictures), writing materials, including A4 paper, board or flip chart, sentence maker.

## PREPARATION

Write key words associated with the Big Book on separate pieces of card (this will depend on the book chosen, but may include: 'eyes', 'mouth', 'tail' and so on).
Make enough copies of photocopiable page 94 for Groups 1 and 2. Make and cut up enough copies of photocopiable page 95 for Group 3.
Write animal names to match the collection of magazine pictures onto card (see also 'Dear Zoo' unit, Hour 1, page 77).

**HOUR 1**

### Introduction

Introduce the non-fiction Big Book. Talk about what is on its cover – the illustration, or photograph, and the title. Ask the children to predict what the book will be about. Then look at the back cover, discuss the picture and read the blurb if there is one.

Now, look through the book, talking about the pictures. Show the children an example of an illustration, which should be about the same subject (ideally, animals). Talk about the differences between the illustration and the photograph, and make sure the children know that the latter is called a photograph. You may like to find a couple of other examples of photographs and illustrations to show them. Explain that non-fiction books usually contain photographs and that we can find out information from these by looking very carefully.

Next, examine one particular photograph and ask the children some questions about it, such as: 'Where would you find this animal?' Encourage the children to think of some questions and write them on the board or flip chart. Talk about the use of question marks as you do this.

### Whole-class skills work

Now, using the prepared key words on card, ask different children to match each word to one in the text, beginning with the title, index and headings. If they are able, they should read the word and the surrounding sentence.

Then, using one of the key words and other common words (these could be taken from a teacher's sentence maker), give one word to each of several children, so that they should be able to stand in a line and make a 'physical sentence'. The rest of the class can help to put them in the right order.

### Differentiated group activities

1*: Carry out a guided read with half of the group, using a set of non-fiction books (or you could use another section of the Big Book). Read the text from the chosen extract together, and examine a photograph carefully, devising suitable questions and finding answers. Meanwhile, the rest of the group should look through a selection of non-fiction books to find books that contain photographs. They might also examine a photograph carefully to see what information it contains so, for example, if it is a photograph of an animal: 'What is the animal doing?' 'Where does it live?'. Exchange tasks after about 10 minutes.

2: Use a selection of non-fiction books to find sentences which contain key words. Write a sentence with a key word and illustrate it.

3: Complete photocopiable page 94, by drawing an animal, where it lives, and what it would eat. Children can refer to posters or books about animals for this information.

### Conclusion

Select a few children to show examples of photographs they have found in books. Encourage them to talk about a chosen photograph and what questions or answers could be gained from it. Group 3 children should show examples of their pictures of animals, with their homes and what they eat. Challenge one child to shuffle the key words and other common words, then try to put them back into a sentence with the rest of the class helping.

### Introduction and whole-class skills work

Remind the children of the non-fiction Big Book used in the previous lesson and the information that can be gained from photographs.

Now, pin a poster of a photograph, or a large photograph from a magazine, onto the board or flip chart. Discuss the photograph, asking questions about the picture, and encouraging the children to say what they want to know about the animal and what the picture tells them. Write some of the key words around the picture. Now ask the children to devise a suitable sentence to describe the picture (tell them that this is called a 'caption'). Write it underneath, talking as you write, for example: 'I must start my sentence with a capital letter and remember to put spaces in between the words. We write the word .... using the letter ... to begin', and so on. Encourage the children to read the sentence back to you.

### Differentiated group activities

1: Use information from photographs to draw pictures of animals, where they live and what they eat (photocopiable page 94). The children should also write the names of the animals, and a sentence about it, if they are able. They may refer to books or posters about animals for this information as in Hour 1.

2*: Guided reading with half of the group using a set of non-fiction books. Read the text from the chosen extract together, and examine a photograph carefully, devising suitable questions and answers. Meanwhile the rest of the group look through a selection of non-fiction books to find books that contain photographs. They might also examine a photograph carefully. Exchange tasks after about 10 minutes.

3: Play Kim's game. Use the words and pictures on photocopiable page 95 (cut out) for this. Encourage the children to look carefully at the pictures, as they will have to recall as many as they can after the pictures are covered up. They should then match word cards to the pictures.

## Conclusion

Select a few children to show the photographs they found in books and discuss the information that can be gained from them. Finish by singing 'Old Macdonald had a farm', giving a number of children cards with the names of animals to hold up so that the rest of the class can read and include these in the song.

# ANIMAL INFORMATION

■ Choose an animal.

■ Draw a picture in each box to match the words.

This animal is a _____

This is where the animal lives.

This is what the animal eats.

# MATCHING ANIMAL WORDS AND PICTURES

| pig | hen | duck |
| horse | cow | cat |
| sheep | goat | mouse |

# PETS

## OBJECTIVES

| UNIT | SPELLING/VOCABULARY | GRAMMAR/PUNCTUATION | COMPREHENSION/ COMPOSITION |
|---|---|---|---|
| WRITING NON-FICTION Information books. | Be able to write own name and explore other words related to spelling of own name. | Write in sentences. Investigate the use of capital letters. | Make own information books including captions to pictures. |

## ORGANIZATION (3 HOURS)

| | INTRODUCTION | WHOLE-CLASS SKILLS WORK | DIFFERENTIATED GROUP ACTIVITIES | CONCLUSION |
|---|---|---|---|---|
| HOUR 1 | Examine format of a non-fiction Big Book. Model making a cover for an information book on pets. | Demonstrate use of capital letters where appropriate. Discuss where capital letters are used and look for examples in texts. | 1*: Guided writing for own information books using template. 2: Sort animal pictures to choose those that would make suitable pets. 3: Use plastic letters to investigate own names. Handwriting practice of names. | Selected pupils show their information books and read examples of captions. Select one child's name and make it with magnetic letters. Investigate other words using the same letters. |
| HOUR 2 | Talk about the class information book and show the cover made in Hour 1. Model making an inside page, with a picture and caption. Model writing captions for pictures which will be included in the class book. | Practise spelling common CVC words using letter names. | 1: Sort animal pictures to choose those that would make suitable pets. Write a list. 2: Use plastic letters to investigate own names. Handwriting practice of names. 3*: Guided writing of own information books using template. | Selected pupils show their information books. Read a caption to a picture and some lists of suitable pets. Whole-class spelling of some pet names (dog, cat) using letter names. |
| HOUR 3 | Read class information book on pets. Model writing further sentences for inclusion. | Talk about the sounds that can be heard at the beginning of different animals' names. Refer to alphabet frieze made in 'Dear Zoo' unit. Play 'Animal I spy'. | 1: Use plastic letters to investigate own names. Look for other words which use the same letters. 2*: Guided writing for own information books using template. 3: Sort animal pictures to choose those that would make suitable pets. | Select pupils show examples of completed information books. Discuss which animals would make the best pets. Talk about which sound can be heard at the beginning of different animals' names and how these would be spelled. |

## RESOURCES

Non-fiction Big Book, a commercially-made blank Big Book or materials for making a Big Book, photocopiable pages 43 (Blank Book Cover from 'Introducing Non-Fiction' unit Term 1) and 99 (Non-fiction Book Template), a selection of animal pictures (taken from magazines), plastic or magnetic letters, the alphabet frieze made in the 'Dear Zoo' unit (see page 79), board or flip chart, writing materials, handwriting books or paper.

## PREPARATION

If necessary make a blank Big Book (see main Introduction, page 10). Make enough copies of photocopiable pages 43 (Blank Book Cover, from Term 1, 'Introducing Non-Fiction' unit) and 99 (Non-fiction Book Template) for one per child.

## HOUR 1

### Introduction

Begin by looking at the format of a non-fiction book, using the sample Big Book. Talk about what is on the front and back covers and point out that pictures and captions are needed inside. (You may refer, in passing, to the Contents and Index pages, but it is not essential to include these in a simple non-fiction book at this stage.)

Now, using the blank Big Book, model putting a front cover together, talking about what you are doing and asking the children to remind you of what is needed. Explain that the book is going to be about pets, but they may like to suggest a more precise title. When you have written the title and the author (Class …), show the children a selection of animal pictures taken from magazines and ask them to choose the best one (or more than one) for the cover.

Next, complete the back cover, including writing a blurb after discussion with the class. A further picture could be chosen for the back.

### Whole-class skills work

While you are modelling the making of a front cover for the non-fiction book, talk about the use of capital letters. Explain that these are used to show when words are important. Then look for examples in a non-fiction Big Book.

### Differentiated group activities

1*: Work with the children on guided writing of non-fiction pet books. Each child should make his or her own book, using photocopiable page 43 for the cover and photocopiable page 99 for the inside pages. Children who are able to write their own titles should do so; others will need extra support. Pictures can either be cut out and stuck down, or children can draw their own. A sentence (for the blurb) should be written on the back cover, with adult help where necessary. Inside the book, there should be a picture on each page with a caption underneath. Provide support for writing the caption, either by writing for the child to copy, or by providing key words.
2: Sort a selection of animal pictures to choose those that would make suitable pets. Children could then choose their preferred pet and draw a picture of it with the name written underneath.
3: Use plastic or magnetic letters to investigate their names. Ask the children to first make their names using the letters, then move the letters around to see if they can make other words. Give the children handwriting books or paper and ask them to practise careful handwriting of their names. If possible they should include both first and second names.

### Conclusion

Select a few children to show their information books and to read examples of their picture captions and blurbs. Select one child's name and make it with plastic or magnetic letters. Then investigate other words that can be made using the same letters.

## HOUR 2

### Introduction

Talk about the class information book and show the cover that was made in Hour 1. Now model making an inside page – with a picture and caption. Talk about writing the caption as you do it, then model writing captions to pictures for inclusion in the class book.

### Whole-class skills work

Use examples of CVC words from the captions you have written to talk about the spelling of these words. Begin by talking about the sounds the children can hear and then talk about the letters used to spell these words, using the letter names. Encourage the children to repeat the spellings, using the letter names.

### Differentiated group activities

1: Sort a selection of pictures to find those that would make suitable pets. The children could then write a list of suitable pets.
2: Use plastic or magnetic letters to investigate their own names and other words that can be made from the same letters. Encourage the children to practise careful handwriting of their names on handwriting books or paper, preferably writing both first and second names.

3\*: Guided writing of individual non-fiction books as in Hour 1, using photocopiable pages 43 and 99. Some children may need an adult to act as a scribe for the captions and blurb.

### Conclusion

Select a few children to show their information books and ask the class to decide if they would guess the title from the picture. Some examples of captions to pictures and lists of suitable pets could also be read out. Follow this with a whole-class spelling of the names of some pets (such as 'dog' or 'cat') using letter names.

### Introduction

Begin by reading the class Big Book on Pets. Talk about the captions to the pictures and model writing a further sentence(s) about a particular pet. Emphasize the use of capital letters at the beginning of a sentence, full stops at the end, and highlight the spelling of CVC words.

### Whole-class skills work

Refer to the alphabet frieze (made during the 'Dear Zoo' unit, see page 79) and talk about the sounds at the beginning of the names of animals. Play a game of 'I spy' using the alphabet frieze.

### Differentiated group activities

1: Use plastic or magnetic letters to investigate their own names and other words that can be made from the same letters. Encourage them to write out lists of the words they have made, emphasizing careful handwriting.

2\*: Guided writing of individual non-fiction books as Groups 1 and 3 in previous hours.

3: Sort a selection of animal pictures to decide on those that would make suitable pets. The children could then choose their ideal pet and draw a picture of it with the name underneath.

### Conclusion

Select children to show examples of their completed information books. Discuss which animals would make the best pets.

Talk about which sound can be heard at the beginning of different animals' names and how these would be spelled (this may be a good opportunity to discuss names such as 'gerbil').

# NON-FICTION BOOK TEMPLATE

Draw a picture in the top box and write a caption in the box below.

# COUNTING RHYMES

## OBJECTIVES

| UNIT | SPELLING/VOCABULARY | GRAMMAR/PUNCTUATION | COMPREHENSION/ COMPOSITION |
|---|---|---|---|
| READING FICTION AND POETRY Counting rhymes and poems. | Explore number rhymes and rhyming words. | Use awareness of sentence structure to help sequence rhymes. | Read traditional, nursery and modern rhymes and poems. |

## ORGANIZATION (5 HOURS)

| | INTRODUCTION | WHOLE-CLASS SKILLS WORK | DIFFERENTIATED GROUP ACTIVITIES | CONCLUSION |
|---|---|---|---|---|
| HOUR 1 | Read 'One, two buckle my shoe' on photocopiable page 104. Teach the actions and practise the rhyme. Read 'One, Two'. Compare versions. | Highlight and compare rhyming words used for numbers. Match a number and rhyming object. Write the number words and rhyming words. | 1*: Guided reading of the poems with half the group. Others listen to number rhymes on tape (exchange). 2: Stick pictures of rhyming objects onto numbers. 3: Sequence lines from 'One, two buckle my shoe'. | Selected pupils show examples of enlarged numbers with rhyming pictures. Pupils read out 'One, two buckle my shoe' correctly sequenced. Whole class re-reads both poems. |
| HOUR 2 | Read the three rhymes and poems on photocopiable page 105. Compare them. | Highlight the rhyming words and compare number rhymes. Talk about alternative rhymes for numbers and compose new version. | 1: Stick pictures of rhyming objects onto numbers. Write rhyming words. 2: Sequence lines from 'One, two, three, four', and 'Two, four, six, eight'. 3*: Guided reading of the poems with half the group. Others listen to number rhymes (exchange). | Selected pupils show numbers with rhyming pictures and words. Pupils read rhyme 'One, two, three, four' correctly sequenced. Re-read different versions of rhymes. |
| HOUR 3 | Read 'Number one, touch your tongue' on photocopiable page 106. Teach actions. Children make a physical number line. | Highlight rhyming words in rhyme. Look at possible alternatives. | 1: Sequence lines from poem. 2*: Guided reading of the poems with half the group. Others listen to number rhymes (exchange). 3: Stick pictures of rhyming objects onto numbers. | Selected pupils show numbers with rhyming pictures and words. Group 1 pupils read the rhyme 'Number one, touch your tongue' correctly sequenced. Re-read the rhyme with actions. Finish by singing 'This old man'. |
| HOUR 4 | Read 'Caribbean Counting Rhyme'. Highlight rhyming words. | Match rhyming words on card to the text. | 1*: Guided reading of the poem with half the group. Others read number rhymes (exchange). 2: Draw pictures of rhyming words for each number from 1 to 10. 3: Play a dice game, matching rhyming pictures to numbers. | Selected pupils show examples of rhyming pictures. Whole class play the dice game. |
| HOUR 5 | Re-read 'Caribbean Counting Rhyme'. Write alternative versions. | Write lists of rhyming words for numbers. | 1: Draw pictures of rhyming words for each number from 1 to 10. 2: Play a dice game matching rhyming pictures to numbers. 3*: Guided reading of the poem with half the group. Others read number rhymes (exchange). | Selected pupils show examples of rhyming pictures. Whole class re-reading of 'Caribbean Counting Rhyme'. |

## RESOURCES

Photocopiable pages 104–107 (various number and counting rhymes) and 108 (Number Rhyming Words and Pictures), a selection of poetry books that contain number rhymes.

Writing materials, including A3 paper, a non-permanent marker pen, adhesive, Blu-Tack.

Large cut-out numbers 1 to 10, A4-size numbers 1 to 10 on card, dice, a selection of objects and pictures of objects that rhyme with the numbers from 1 to 10, a box or bag.

A listening centre, headphones, number rhymes on tape.

## PREPARATION

Make enlarged copies of all the counting rhymes on photocopiable pages 104–107 (possibly blanking out the actions for 'One, two buckle my shoe') and laminate these if possible. Alternatively, type the words onto a computer in a 48 point font and print.

Make extra copies of the rhymes 'One, two buckle my shoe' (photocopiable page 104), 'One, two, three, four' and 'Two, four, six, eight' (photocopiable page 105) and 'Number one, touch your tongue' (photocopiable page 106) and cut them into separate lines.

Write the rhyming words from 'Caribbean Counting Rhyme' (photocopiable page 107) on card.

Divide A3 paper into ten sections, and head each of the sections with a number 1 to 10. Make enough copies for two groups.

### Introduction

Read from the enlarged version of 'One, two buckle my shoe' (photocopiable page 104) pointing to the words as you read. Teach the children the actions to the rhyme as shown on the photocopiable sheet and practise these. Now read 'One, two' on the same page and compare the two versions. Highlight the words that rhyme with the numbers on both versions.

### Whole-class skills work

Now ask a child to select a number from the cards and then choose a rhyming object (these could be in a box or bag). The rest of the class should decide whether the object rhymes with the number word. When you have covered all the numbers from 1 to 10, write each number word, and the corresponding rhyming word, on the board.

### Differentiated group activities

1*: Carry out a guided read of the enlarged versions of the rhymes on photocopiable page 104 with half of the group, emphasizing the rhyming words. Meanwhile the rest of the group should listen to a selection of number rhymes on a tape (commercial or home-made) using a listening centre and headphones. Exchange tasks after about 10 minutes.
2: Give the children the large cut-out numbers and ask them to stick corresponding rhyming pictures on to the number, so a picture of a sun on '1', a picture of a shoe on '2', and so on. Use photocopiable page 108 to help explain the task.
3: Re-assemble cut-up lines from 'One, two buckle my shoe'. The children should then compare their lines with a printed version and say the rhyme.

### Conclusion

Select a few children to show examples of enlarged numbers with rhyming pictures. Some Group 3 children could read out 'One, two buckle my shoe' correctly sequenced. Finally, re-read both poems with the whole class and compare the rhyming words.

### Introduction

Read the enlarged version of the 'One, two, three, four' and 'Two, four, six, eight' rhymes (from photocopiable page 105). Discuss the rhyming number words and then read the final poem on the page, 'Telling' by Wendy Cope, pointing at the words as you read. Compare 'One, two, three, four' and 'Telling' and discuss how the poems have different meanings because of the changes in the words.

### Whole-class skills work

Highlight the rhyming words by underlining them and compare the different rhymes in the three poems. Ask the children to suggest alternative rhymes and help them compose their own versions.

### Differentiated group activities

1: Find pictures of things that rhyme with numbers and stick these on to the corresponding enlarged cut-out number. Write a list of rhyming words next to each number. Photocopiable page 108 might be used to explain the task.
2: Re-assemble cut-up lines from 'One, two, three, four' and 'Two, four, six, eight'. The children should then compare their sequenced lines with a printed version and say the rhyme.
3*: Carry out a guided read of the enlarged versions of the rhymes with half of the group, emphasizing the rhyming words. Meanwhile the rest of the group listen to a selection of number rhymes on tape using a listening centre and headphones. Exchange tasks after about 10 minutes.

### Conclusion

Select children to show numbers with rhyming pictures and words. Ask some Group 2 children to read the rhyme 'One, two, three, four' correctly sequenced. The whole class can then re-read the different versions of the rhymes.

### Introduction

Read 'Number one, touch your tongue' (photocopiable page 106), pointing to the enlarged version as you are reading. Re-read it with the children joining in, then teach them the actions.

Choose different children to hold up the number cards from 1 to 10 and make a physical number line in the correct order. Say the rhyme again with the class, asking the children to hold up their numbers at the appropriate time, while the rest of the class says the rhyme with the actions.

### Whole-class skills work

Examine the rhyming words by underlining them on the enlarged, laminated version of the poem. Ask the children to suggest possible alternatives.

### Differentiated group activities

1: Sequence lines from 'Number one, touch your tongue', then write out the correctly-sequenced poem.
2*: Carry out a guided read of the enlarged versions of the rhymes with half of the group, emphasizing the rhyming words. Meanwhile the rest of the group listen to a selection of number rhymes on tape using a listening centre and headphones. Exchange tasks after about 10 minutes.
3: Stick corresponding rhyming pictures on enlarged cut-out numbers. Photocopiable page 108 might be helpful for this.

### Conclusion

Choose a few children to show their numbers with rhyming pictures. Group 1 children could read the rhyme 'Number one, touch your tongue' correctly sequenced. Then re-read the rhyme with the whole class doing the accompanying actions. Finish by singing 'This old man'.

### Introduction

Read the enlarged, laminated version of 'Caribbean Counting Rhyme' (photocopiable page 107), pointing to the words as you read. Then re-read the poem with the children joining in. Highlight the rhyming words by underlining them.

### Whole-class skills work

Show the children the rhyming words from the poem that you have written on card. Ask different individuals to match these to the poem, then try to read them.

### Differentiated group activities

1*: Carry out a guided read of the poem with half of the group. If the rhyming words have been masked with Blu-Tack, the children can try to guess which word fits. The rest of the group should look at a selection of poetry books to find further examples of number rhymes. Exchange tasks after about 10 minutes.

2: Draw pictures to rhyme with the numbers from 1 to 10, on A3 paper.

3: Play a dice game. Players take turns to throw a dice numbered 1 to 6 and then choose a picture to rhyme with the number thrown from a selection provided. The person with the most pictures at the end wins.

### Conclusion

Select a few children to show examples of rhyming pictures for the numbers from 1 to 10. Play the dice game with the whole class, preferably with a large dice.

**HOUR 5**

### Introduction and whole-class skills work

Read the enlarged version of 'Caribbean Counting Rhyme' (photocopiable page 107). Write lists of different rhyming words for each number from 1 to 10. Now discuss new alternative versions of the poem, possibly something like: 'One by one, one by one, children having lots of fun.' The lists of rhyming words will help to provide suggestions.

### Differentiated group activities

1: On A3 paper draw pictures to rhyme with the numbers from 1 to 10 and write the words underneath.

2: Play the dice game, as in Hour 4. Players throw a dice numbered 1 to 6 and choose a corresponding rhyming picture for the number they have thrown from a selection.

3*: Guided read of the poem with half of the group, while the others look at a selection of poetry books to find further examples of number rhymes. Exchange tasks after about 10 minutes.

### Conclusion

Select some children to show examples of rhyming pictures. Finish with a whole-class re-reading of 'Caribbean Counting Rhyme' and a discussion of alternative versions.

# NUMBER RHYMES: 1

**One, Two Buckle My Shoe**

One, two buckle my shoe;

Three, four knock at the door;

Five, six pick up sticks;

Seven, eight lay them straight;

Nine, ten a big fat hen;

Eleven, twelve dig and delve;

Thirteen, fourteen maids a-courting;

Fifteen, sixteen maids in the kitchen;

Seventeen, eighteen maids in waiting;

Nineteen, twenty my plate's empty.

*Traditional*

**One, Two**

One, two,
Where are you?

Three, four,
Behind the door?

Five, six,
Playing tricks.

Seven, eight,
Found you, mate!

Nine, ten,
Let's play again.

*Anonymous*

# NUMBER RHYMES: 2

**One, two, three, four**

One, two, three, four,

Mary's at the cottage door;

Five, six, seven, eight,

Eating cherries off a plate.

*Traditional*

**Two, four, six, eight**

Two, four, six, eight,

Meet me at the garden gate.

If I'm late, don't wait,

Two, four, six, eight.

*Anonymous*

**Telling**

One, two, three, four,

Telling Miss that Gary swore.

Five, six, seven, eight,

Now I haven't got a mate.

*Wendy Cope*

# NUMBER RHYMES: 3

**Number one, touch your tongue**

Number one, touch your tongue.

Number two, touch your shoe.

Number three, touch your knee.

Number four, touch the floor.

Number five, learn to jive.

Number six, pick up sticks.

Number seven, point to heaven.

Number eight, shut the gate.

Number nine, touch your spine.

Number ten, do it again!

*Julia Matthews*

# NUMBER RHYMES: 4

## Caribbean Counting Rhyme

One by one
one by one
waves are dancing
in the sun.

Two by two
two by two
seashells pink
and purply-blue.

Three by three
three by three
big boats
putting out to sea.

Four by four
four by four
children fishing
on the shore.

Five by five
five by five
little walking
fish arrive.

Six by six
six by six
pelicans
performing tricks.

Seven by seven
seven by seven
puffy clouds
patrolling heaven.

Eight by eight
eight by eight
fishes nibbling
juicy bait.

Nine by nine
nine by nine
taking home
a catch that's fine.

Ten by ten
ten by ten
tomorrow we
will come again.

*Pamela Mordecai*

# NUMBER RHYMING WORDS AND PICTURES

# TWINKLE TWINKLE CHOCOLATE BAR

## OBJECTIVES

| UNIT | SPELLING/VOCABULARY | GRAMMAR/PUNCTUATION | COMPREHENSION/ COMPOSITION |
|---|---|---|---|
| WRITING FICTION AND POETRY Cumulative and repetitive poems: *Twinkle Twinkle Chocolate Bar* compiled by John Foster. | Find words with the c/k initial letter sound. Investigate onset and rimes (-ar, -at, -all, -ay). Identify letter patterns in words that rhyme. | Highlight repeated refrains. | Write shared poems substituting words and phrases from poems read. |

## ORGANIZATION (5 HOURS)

| | INTRODUCTION | WHOLE-CLASS SKILLS WORK | DIFFERENTIATED GROUP ACTIVITIES | CONCLUSION |
|---|---|---|---|---|
| HOUR 1 | Read the poem 'Twinkle Twinkle Chocolate Bar' (Anon.) and compare with 'Twinkle, Twinkle Little Star'. | Highlight rhyming words, looking at -ar rime. Use plastic or magnetic letters to demonstrate how to change the onset and make different words. | 1*: Guided writing of alternative version of 'Twinkle, Twinkle Little Star'. 2: Use plastic letters to investigate -ar rime words by changing onsets. 3: Play dominoes with rhyming pictures. | Discuss alternative rhymes that have been written. Show lists of words with -ar rime. Demonstrate rhyming dominoes game with the whole class. |
| HOUR 2 | Read the poem 'Lost and Found' (J. Kitching). Highlight repeated phrases. | Underline rhyming words and substitute alternative words to rhyme with names of pupils in the class. | 1: Play dominoes with rhyming words. 2*: Guided writing of verses of poem similar to 'Lost and Found'. 3: Use plastic letters to investigate -ar rime words by changing onsets. | Selected pupils read out different verses to poem. Discuss words that sound the same but do not share the same spelling (rime). |
| HOUR 3 | Read 'this is the key to the castle' (Dave Calder). Talk about how the poem builds up as more and more lines are added. Underline the repeated phrases. | Discuss the sound made by the letters c and k and look at words beginning with this sound. | 1*: Re-write verses to 'this is the key to the castle'. 2: Listen to the poem on tape while reading the text. 3: Track words which use the k/c sound in newspapers or magazines. | Selected Group 1 pupils read out alternative versions of the poem. Group 3 pupils share examples of words beginning with the k/c sound. Whole class repeats the refrain from the poem. |
| HOUR 4 | Re-read 'this is the key to the castle', underlining rhyming words in each verse. Discuss similarities with 'The House that Jack Built'. | Identify words that rhyme with the same letter patterns. Use magnetic letters to make further words by changing the onsets. | 1: Use plastic letters to investigate -at, -all and -ay rime words by changing onsets. Write a list. 2*: Re-write verses to 'this is the key to the castle'. 3: Listen to the poem on tape while reading text. | Selected pupils show words using -at, -all and -ay rimes and examples of alternative verses. Whole class practises the repeated refrains. |
| HOUR 5 | Re-read ' 'The House that Jack Built', this time choosing pupils to act out the various parts with the rest of the class saying the refrain. | Investigate further words which use the rimes -all and -ay. | 1: Listen to the poem on tape while reading the text. 2: Use plastic letters to investigate -at, -all and -ay rime words by changing onsets. 3*: Write verses to 'The House that Jack Built'. | Selected pupils show examples of words using -at, -all, -ay rimes. Perform the poem. |

## RESOURCES

One, or more, copies of the poetry anthology *Twinkle Twinkle Chocolate Bar* compiled by John Foster (Oxford University Press, ISBN 0-19-276125-0), photocopiable pages 113 (Rhyming Domino Pictures) and 114 and 115 ('The House that Jack Built').

Plastic or magnetic letters, card, rhyming pictures to make rhyming dominoes, a selection of pages cut from magazines or newspapers, a non-permanent marker pen.

A board or flip chart, a tape recorder and headphones, a selection of objects that begin with the sound *k*, a computer (optional).

## PREPARATION

Make, and laminate, enlarged versions of the poems 'Twinkle Twinkle Chocolate Bar' (Anon.), 'Lost and Found' by J. Kitching and 'this is the key to the castle' by Dave Calder – from *Twinkle Twinkle Chocolate Bar* – and the traditional rhyme 'Twinkle Twinkle Little Star. Either photocopy the poems once and enlarge, or type them out on a computer using 48 point size font. Photocopy and enlarge photocopiable pages 114 and 115 ('The House that Jack Built').

Write the words from the poem 'Twinkle Twinkle Chocolate Bar' on separate cards, as well as a selection of alternative words which use the -*ar* rime, such as: bar, car, jar, tar, star, far.

Make rhyming dominoes by sticking a selection of rhyming pictures onto card and laminating. You could use photocopiable page 67 from 'The Gingerbread Man: 2' unit (Term 1) for this as well as the pictures on photocopiable page 113. Make a home-made tape of the poem 'this is the key to the castle'.

### Introduction and whole-class skills work

Read the enlarged version of 'Twinkle Twinkle Chocolate Bar', pointing to the words. Compare this with 'Twinkle Twinkle Little Star', looking particularly at the words that have changed. Highlight the words which rhyme and, using plastic or magnetic letters, talk about the -*ar* rime and make different words by changing the onset.

### Differentiated group activities

1*: Guided writing of alternative versions of 'Twinkle, Twinkle Little Star'. Give the children the words from the poem 'Twinkle Twinkle Chocolate Bar' on separate cards as well as the alternative words for the -*ar* rime (bar, car, jar, far, and so on) and ask them to reorder the words to make a poem. Encourage them to write out their final versions of the poem.
2: Use plastic or magnetic letters to investigate -*ar* rime words by changing onsets. Children might then write a list of words, drawing a picture for each one.
3: Play rhyming dominoes, with the aim of matching two rhyming pictures.

### Conclusion

Select one or two children to talk about the alternative rhymes that have been written. These could later be included in a class book of rhymes. Group 2 children might also show their lists of words which use the -*ar* rime. Finish by allowing the whole class to take part in a rhyming dominoes game. They should sit in a circle and take turns to choose a card, then see if it will rhyme with one already laid down.

### Introduction and whole-class skills work

Read 'Lost and Found' by J. Kitching, using an enlarged version so that the whole class can see the print clearly. Highlight repeated phrases and underline rhyming words.

Then try substituting the names of children in the class to make a lost and found poem, such as: 'Jonathan Bates, lost his mates, couldn't find them, behind the gates.' Or 'Anna Brown, lost her gown, found it in the middle of town.'

### Differentiated group activities

1: Play rhyming dominoes and extend, if appropriate, by using the words on reverse side of the pictures.
2*: Guided writing of alternative verses for a 'Lost and Found' poem using the names of children in the class. Each child should write a verse for his or her own name.

3: Use plastic or magnetic letters to investigate -ar rime words by changing onsets. Provide lists of possible words as a support.

### Conclusion
Ask a few children to read out different verses to the poem that fit their names. This may be a good opportunity to discuss words that sound the same but do not share the same spelling (rime).

### Introduction
Read the enlarged version of the poem 'this is the key to the castle' by Dave Calder to the class, possibly using this as an opportunity to make a recording of the poem. Point to each word as you read it.

Re-read the poem, but this time ask the children to join in the repeated refrains. Talk about how the poem builds up as more and more lines are added. Underline the repeated phrases on the enlarged, laminated version.

### Whole-class skills work
Discuss the sound made by the first letter in 'key' and 'castle' and ask for further suggestions of words that begin with this sound (you might like to reinforce this by looking at a selection of objects which begin with the sound). You could look at the other spelling choices for this sound – ck (as in duck), ch (as in school) and q (as in queen).

### Differentiated group activities
1*: Re-write the verses to 'this is the key to the castle', substituting alternative nouns. (This could be done on the computer, or you could print out verses from the poem leaving some of the nouns blank.)
2: Listen to the poem on tape, following it at the same time in a book. Encourage the children to learn sections of it for later performance.
3: Track words which use the k/c sound in newspapers or magazines, highlighting any that are found.

### Conclusion
Select some children to read out alternative verses of the poem. Ask a few Group 3 children to share examples of words beginning with the k/c sound. The whole class can then repeat the refrain from the poem.

### Introduction and whole-class skills work
Re-read 'this is the key to the castle', emphasizing, and then underlining, the rhyming words in each verse. Talk about the similarities with 'The House that Jack Built' (photocopiable pages 114 and 115). Identify words that rhyme with the same letter patterns, such as: fat/ sat, hall/wall, play/day. Use plastic or magnetic letters to make further words by changing the onsets.

### Differentiated group activities
1: Use plastic or magnetic letters to investigate -at, -all and -ay rime words by changing onsets. Write each different rime on the board or on a card. Children should write out lists of the words they have made.
2*: Re-write the verses to 'this is the key to the castle', substituting alternative nouns.
3: Listen to the poem on tape, at the same time following it on the enlarged version. Encourage the children to try to learn the refrain for a later performance.

### Conclusion
Group 1 children should show the words with -at, -all and -ay rimes that they have made. Examples of alternative verses should be shown too. Finish with the whole class practising the repeated refrain.

### Introduction and whole-class skills work
Re-read 'The House that Jack Built' on photocopiable pages 114 and 115, this time

choosing individual children to act out the various parts, with the rest of the class saying the refrain. Continue to use plastic letters to investigate words with -all and -ay rimes.

### Differentiated group activities

1: Listen to the poem on tape, following it in the book at the same time. The children should aim to learn sections for later performance.

2: Use plastic or magnetic letters to investigate -at, -all and -ay rime words by changing onsets. Put each different rime on a card, or write them on the board. The children should write out lists of the words they make.

3*: Re-write the verses to 'The House that Jack Built', substituting alternative nouns. Rhyming cards and pictures might be used to help the children find alternative rhymes.

### Conclusion

Select a few Group 2 children to show examples of their lists of -at, -all and -ay rimes. Finish with a further practice of a performance of the poem by the whole class with different children taking parts and everyone joining in the refrain.

# RHYMING DOMINO PICTURES

# THE HOUSE THAT JACK BUILT

This is the house that Jack built.

This is the malt that lay in the house that Jack built.

This is the rat that ate the malt, that lay in the house that Jack built.

This is the cat that chased the rat, that ate the malt, that lay in the house that Jack built.

This is the dog that worried the cat, that chased the rat, that ate the malt, that lay in the house that Jack built.

This is the cow with the crumpled horn, that tossed the dog, that worried the cat, that chased the rat, that ate the malt, that lay in the house that Jack built.

This is the maiden all forlorn, that milked the cow with the crumpled horn, that tossed the dog, that worried the cat, that chased the rat, that ate the malt, that lay in the house that Jack built.

# THE HOUSE THAT JACK BUILT (CONT'D)

This is the man all tattered and torn, that kissed the maiden all forlorn, that milked the cow with the crumpled horn, that tossed the dog, that worried the cat, that chased the rat, that ate the malt, that lay in the house that Jack built.

This is the priest all shaven and shorn, that married the man all tattered and torn, that kissed the maiden all forlorn, that milked the cow with the crumpled horn, that tossed the dog, that worried the cat, that chased the rat, that ate the malt, that lay in the house that Jack built.

This is the cock that crowed in the morn, that waked the priest all shaven and shorn, that married the man all tattered and torn, that kissed the maiden all forlorn, that milked the cow with the crumpled horn, that tossed the dog, that worried the cat, that chased the rat, that ate the malt, that lay in the house that Jack built.

This is the farmer sowing his corn, that kept the cock that crowed in the morn, that waked the priest all shaven and shorn, that married the man all tattered and torn, that kissed the maiden all forlorn, that milked the cow with the crumpled horn, that tossed the dog, that worried the cat, that chased the rat, that ate the malt, that lay in the house that Jack built.

# ALL KINDS OF FOOD

## OBJECTIVES

| UNIT | SPELLING/VOCABULARY | GRAMMAR/PUNCTUATION | COMPREHENSION/ COMPOSITION |
|------|---------------------|---------------------|----------------------------|
| READING NON-FICTION Simple non-fiction texts: Advertisements. | Identify and write initial and dominant phonemes in spoken words. Identify letter patterns in words. | Be aware of the use of capital letters for proper nouns. | Recognize printed and handwritten words in a variety of settings. Read words in advertisements. Locate print in the environment. Identify brand names. |

## ORGANIZATION (5 HOURS)

| | INTRODUCTION | WHOLE-CLASS SKILLS WORK | DIFFERENTIATED GROUP ACTIVITIES | CONCLUSION |
|--|--------------|------------------------|--------------------------------|------------|
| HOUR 1 | Look at a scrapbook of assorted packaging from food. 'Read' the brand names. Discuss where you could buy these products. | Look carefully at the names of the products and talk about the sounds at the beginning of the words. Ask the children to show you how to write the letters. | 1*: Guided reading of assorted food packaging with half the group. Others sort food packaging (exchange). 2: Make scrapbooks of food packaging in categories. 3: Put products on correct shelves in class shop. | Selected pupils show their scrapbooks and the tidy class shop. Read further examples of food packaging emphasizing phonic cues. |
| HOUR 2 | Take class walk in the environment to look at examples of advertising. Take some photographs. | Look at examples of advertising leaflets. Talk about which shop they came from. Write sentences using brand names. | 1: Make scrapbooks of food packaging, in categories. Add labels. 2: Put products on correct shelves in the class shop. 3*: Guided reading of assorted food packaging with half the group. Others sort food packaging (exchange). | Selected pupils show their scrapbooks and examples of favourite products. Shared writing of sentences about favourite products for the class to read. |
| HOUR 3 | Display silhouette shapes of a row of shops. Ask the children to stick a range of signs in the appropriate places. | Identify letter patterns on some familiar packaging, such as the ar in 'Mars'. Look for further examples. | 1: Put products on correct shelves in the class shop. 2*: Guided reading of assorted food packaging with half the group. Others sort food packaging (exchange). 3: Make scrapbooks of food packaging. | Show examples of scrapbooks. Identify further letter patterns in brand names and packaging. |
| HOUR 4 | Read from the class scrapbook of advertisements. Write labels for the scrapbook for the children to read. | Use a shopping basket containing a selection of objects which begin with the same initial sound to emphasize the sound. Write the words on the board. | 1: Use shopping baskets to collect items that begin with the same sound from the class shop. 2*: Identify capital letters on advertisements and read the words. 3: Play a lotto game. | Show shopping baskets so the class can check if items begin with the same sound. Teacher writes up the names of the items that begin with the same sound. Discuss use of capital letters on advertisements. |
| HOUR 5 | Oral cloze with sentences relating to a shopping trip – 'I was going down the street when I saw a sign for...'. | Play 'I spy' with items from the class shop. | 1: Lotto game with different brand names where the correct labels have to be placed on top. 2: Collect items that begin with the same sound from class shop. 3*: Oral cloze, then write sentences. | Show examples of shopping baskets and write lists of items that begin with the same sound. Whole-class reading of sentences written by Group 3. |

## RESOURCES

A scrapbook filled with various types of assorted well-known food packaging and labels (you will need a large supply of these materials so it would be a good idea to ask the children to collect these and bring them in from home in advance), further food packaging and advertising leaflets, individual scrapbooks, photocopiable page121 (What a Lotto Food!).

Props for a class food shop including bags or baskets, labels for shelves and other suitable signs, further labels with categories of food for sorting activities, a wall display showing silhouettes of shops (see illustration and Preparation, below).

Shopping baskets filled with objects which all have the same initial sound, plastic or magnetic letters, a yellow felt-tipped pen, a board or flip chart, a camera with film.

## PREPARATION

Buy, or make, an A3 class scrapbook. Include a title page, headed 'All Kinds of Food', and group different types of food labels onto facing pages (packaging from cereal packets, sweets, chocolate, fast food, fish, meat, vegetables, fruit). Leave space for labels and sentences to be added.

Make individual scrapbooks (A4 size) for the children – plain exercise books could be used for this. Write a list of categories of types of products for children to copy. Make several large labels for the shop and for sorting products into categories.

Make a display of the silhouette of a row of shops on one wall or area in the classroom (see illustration below). Simple outlines can be cut out from different coloured sugar paper and a selection of suitable pictures stuck onto each 'shop' (fruit and vegetables on the greengrocer's shop, sweets on the sweet shop, meat on the butcher's shop, a selection of groceries on the supermarket). Leave a space for a shop sign to be added and prepare a suitably sized sign (this could be printed on the computer, then stuck onto card to be fixed to the display later with Blu-Tack).

Make a lotto game (see example below) by printing or writing different brand names of products (for which you have labels) onto each section of a board divided into six rectangles (see photocopiable page 121). Be sure to put the product names in different places on each board so the children cannot copy each other. The game is then played with a set of corresponding brand labels.

**What a lotto food!**

| Don's Dairy Milk | Grandma Spicer's Sweets | Porky Pork Pies |
|---|---|---|
| Old Farmhouse Cheese | Freezo Garden Peas | Wake Up Coffee |

### Introduction

Show the children the large scrapbook you have made of different types of food packaging. Ask them if they know what any of the writing says – they will all be able to read the names of their own favourite restaurants and foodstuffs. Discuss where the different types of food could be bought and ensure that all the children are familiar with different types of shops, such as butchers or bakers.

### Whole-class skills work

Look carefully at one or two product names and say the names aloud, emphasizing the initial sounds. Ask the children to identify which sound they can hear and to say the name of the letter(s) used for writing this sound. Choose different children to write the correct letter, on the board or flip chart, in response to the sound. This might be extended by asking children to identify sounds at the end of words, and any other dominant phoneme.

### Differentiated group activities

1*: Read an assortment of food packaging and labels with half the group while the rest of the group sorts food packaging into categories and puts the correct label next to each: 'vegetables', 'sweets' and so on. Exchange tasks after about 10 minutes.
2: Make individual scrapbooks of food labels, which are sorted into categories (as in the large example used in the Introduction). Provide a list of categories, such as 'Sweets' or 'Cereal', so that children can copy these headings into their scrapbooks.
3: Sort a collection of products (empty packets, boxes, and so on) onto the correct shelves of the class shop. Different sections or shelves should be labelled accordingly. If space allows you could also hang signs, similar to those seen in supermarkets, from the ceiling above the correct spot.

### Conclusion

Group 2 children can show their individual scrapbooks and read the labels they have written. The rest of the class can check if they are labelled correctly. Ask one child to go into the class shop and find the 'Sweets' sign – were the sweets in the right place? Read one or two further examples of packaging with the children and emphasize how the sounds of the letters help us to read the words.

### Introduction

Take the children for a walk, preferably somewhere where they can see a row of shops. If you do not have local shops, you may need to plan a separate visit to show the children examples of print in the environment. While you are out, take any opportunities to point out examples of advertising (and ask other adult helpers to do the same). Read any signs you see and check how many are familiar to the children.

Take plenty of photographs for later display in the classroom. If you are unable to do this, you may have to rely on published photographs and pictures, but this does not replace the value of first-hand experience.

### Whole-class skills work

In the classroom, talk about all the signs you have seen and look at examples of advertising leaflets. Talk about the different shops each leaflet came from – ideally the children will have collected them on their walk. Now, ensuring that the children can read the brand names on the advertising leaflets, write a suitable sentence on the board or flip chart (eg, 'We play with Lego' or 'We like Cadbury's chocolate') for them to read. As you do so, talk about using capital letters for proper nouns.

### Differentiated group activities

1: Make individual scrapbooks of food labels, which are sorted into categories. Provide a list of categories so the children can write the correct labels in their scrapbooks. Provide a more extensive range and list for this group.
2: Sort a collection of products in the class shop (empty packets, boxes, and so on) onto the correctly labelled shelves.
3*: Read a restricted assortment of food packaging and labels with half the group while the rest of the group sorts food packaging into categories. Exchange tasks after about 10 minutes.

## Conclusion

Ask a few Group 1 children to show examples of their individual scrapbooks to the class and discuss the labelling. Choose one or two children to select their favourite products from the class shop. Write a sentence for each product on the board or flip chart for the class to read, and ask the children why you used capital letters in certain places.

## Introduction

Talk about the classroom display of a row of shops. Ask one child to go and point to the baker's shop or butcher's shop. Ensure that the children know what kinds of things they will find in the different shops. Now show them the shop signs you have made and choose children to read the signs and then fix them to the correct 'shop' on the display.

## Whole-class skills work

Look at examples of food packaging and explain to the children that you are going on a letter hunt and the letters you are looking for are, for example, *ar*. Show them an item that corresponds (for *ar* it might be a Mars bar).

Try to find one or two examples for the same letter pattern and talk about the sound these letters make. In the case of a Mars bar, you can make the words with plastic or magnetic letters and show how the change in onset changes the word.

## Differentiated group activities

1: Sort a collection of products in the class shop (empty packets, boxes and so on) onto the correctly labelled shelves. Add additional labels and products for this group.
2*: Read an assortment of food packaging and labels with half the group while the rest of the group sorts food packaging into categories and adds some labels. Exchange tasks after about 10 minutes.
3: Make individual scrapbooks of food labels, which are sorted into categories. Assist the children to write the correct labels in their scrapbooks. You may need to write these in yellow felt-tipped pen to be traced over, with the starting point for each letter marked, depending on the ability of the children in the group.

## Conclusion

Show examples of individual scrapbooks to the class and look at sorted examples of packaging. Using some of these labels, ask the children to help you go on a letter hunt. Write the letters you are seeking on the board (choose some where you can find several examples, perhaps *ish*) and ask the children to help you identify the labels that match.

## Introduction

Read examples of food packaging from the large class scrapbook, then write some labels to match the types of food. You might also add some sentences, such as: 'You buy chocolate in a sweet shop.' 'You buy meat in a butcher's shop.' This may be a good opportunity to discuss that all these products can be bought in a 'supermarket' as well.

## Whole-class skills work

Show the class the prepared shopping basket and explain that these are things you bought earlier. Pick up the goods, one at a time, and see if the children notice that they all begin with the same sound. (Emphasize the sound as you say each word.) Write the words for the different products on the board or flip chart, talking about the letters used.

## Differentiated group activities

1: Give each member of the group a shopping bag or basket and ask them to collect items that begin with the same sound from the class shop. They could also write a shopping list of the collected items.
2*: Identify examples of capital letters on advertisements and read the words. Write lists of words that begin with the same letter.
3: Play a lotto game using the lotto boards from photocopiable page 121 – write brand names or stick food labels on each board. For this group you could draw pictures to accompany the food names. The children take turns to take a food label from a pile in the middle of the table and see if they have the corresponding word on their board. If so, they place a counter on it. The first person to cover all their board is the winner.

### Conclusion
Ask a few children to show examples of their shopping baskets, taking out the items so the class can see if they all begin with the same sound. On the board or flip chart you might write the names of the items that begin with the same sound. Discuss the use of capital letters and ask some Group 2 children to show examples on advertisements.

### Introduction
Play an oral cloze game with the class, using advertisements as the stimulus. If possible, use the photographs you took earlier in the week (Hour 2). For example: 'I was going down the street when I saw a sign for something beginning with s (sweets).' Use the pictures in the scrapbook to reinforce this.

### Whole-class skills work
Play a game of 'I spy' using items from the class shop. Write up the letter on the board or flip chart as well as saying it, then follow this by writing the word, once it has been guessed.

### Differentiated group activities
1: Play the lotto game using the prepared lotto boards that have brand names on. Provide a wider selection of food labels for this group to read.
2: Collect items that begin with the same sound from the class shop using shopping baskets.
3*: Play an oral cloze game, as in the Introduction, using common food items. Write corresponding sentences for the group to read.

### Conclusion
Look at further examples of shopping baskets and check whether items begin with the same sound. Who collected most items in his or her basket? Read some of the sentences written with Group 3 with the whole class.

# What a lotto food!

# DON'T FORGET THE BACON!

## OBJECTIVES

| UNIT | SPELLING/VOCABULARY | GRAMMAR/PUNCTUATION | COMPREHENSION/ COMPOSITION |
|---|---|---|---|
| WRITING NON-FICTION Lists, labels and sentences about food. | Match words to pictures on lists. Use packaging labels to copy words for lists. Consider the initial sounds of words. | Complete sentences using sentence frames. Use capital letters for proper nouns. | Write shopping lists. Complete sentences for favourite foods. Make posters. |

## ORGANIZATION (5 HOURS)

| | INTRODUCTION | WHOLE-CLASS SKILLS WORK | DIFFERENTIATED GROUP ACTIVITIES | CONCLUSION |
|---|---|---|---|---|
| HOUR 1 | Read *Don't Forget the Bacon!* by Pat Hutchins. Discuss the problem of going shopping and trying to remember several items. | Model writing a list using items from story. Demonstrate the use of food labels (mounted on card) to help in writing words for lists. | 1*: Guided reading of *Don't Forget the Bacon!* with half the group. Others write shopping lists using emergent writing (exchange). 2: Use food labels to write shopping lists. 3: Role-play in class shop using prepared lists. | Selected pupils show their shopping lists. The rest of the class see if they can read the lists. One pupil could actually buy the items in the class shop. |
| HOUR 2 | Use *Don't Forget the Bacon!* to remind the children of the need for lists. Model writing a list for items in the class shop. Use a mixture of drawings and writing. | Examine carefully the words that change in *Don't Forget the Bacon!* Talk about the way in which the words are similar (they rhyme) and which letters change. | 1: Write lists and then use them to 'buy' the items in the class shop. 2*: Guided reading of *Don't Forget the Bacon!* with half the group. Others use plastic letters to investigate -*ake* rime words by changing onsets (exchange). 3: Use food labels to write shopping lists. | Show examples of shopping lists. Investigate different onsets with -*ake* rime. |
| HOUR 3 | Discuss favourite foods, matching pupils' names to food labels. Talk about healthy foods. Model making a simple poster about healthy food. | Talk about when to use capital letters (for the names of products). Look for examples. | 1: Cut out pictures of healthy foods to make into posters. 2: Sort collections of pictures into healthy and unhealthy foods. 3*: Write individual books entitled 'I like'. | Show examples of 'I like' books and posters of healthy foods. Discuss which foods are healthy. Look for examples of capital letters and reinforce their purpose. |
| HOUR 4 | Read examples of different shopping lists with the whole class. Choose different pupils to 'buy' the items. | Play a game of 'I went to market and I bought ...' only using items that begin with a chosen letter. | 1: Sort pictures into healthy and unhealthy foods and write the words. 2*: Write individual books entitled 'I like'. 3: Cut out pictures of healthy foods to make into posters. | Selected pupils show examples of pictures for posters and individual 'I like' books. Using pictures of different foods, write lists of healthy foods for the class to read. |
| HOUR 5 | Discuss pupils' favourite foods, using a collection of chocolate bar wrappers. Model writing sentences, using sentence frames: 'I like... but I don't like...' | Talk about the sound *ch* as in 'chocolate'. Explain that the two letters make one sound (a digraph). Collect other examples of words that have this sound. | 1*: Write individual books entitled 'I like', adding 'but I don't like...' 2: Cut out pictures of healthy foods to make into posters. Add writing. 3: Sort *ch* pictures from a selection. | Selected pupils show examples of individual books and posters. Finish by putting objects which begin with *ch* into a shopping basket. |

## RESOURCES
Copies of *Don't Forget the Bacon!* by Pat Hutchins (Picture Puffin, ISBN 0-14-050315-3), photocopiable page 126 (Healthy Food – Or Not?).
A collection of assorted food labels, including chocolate bar wrappers, assorted pictures of food from magazines, a selection of objects and pictures of food items beginning with *ch* (such as: chocolate, cheese, chips, cherries, chops, chicken), props for the class shop.
Writing materials, including A3, A4, white and coloured, and A5 paper for shopping lists, card (including children's name cards), plastic or magnetic letters, board or flip chart.

## PREPARATION

Mount a selection of food labels onto card or write the names of the food items from *Don't Forget the Bacon!* (eggs, cake, pears and bacon) onto card with a picture of each item either cut from a magazine or drawn.
Make individual 'I like' books by folding A4 coloured paper in half, with several sheets of white A4 paper inside.
Set up the class shop with suitable props, including shopping baskets, a till and signs. Write a selection of shopping lists on A5 paper. Make enough copies of photocopiable page 126 (Healthy Food – Or Not?) for two groups.

## SYNOPSIS

*Don't Forget the Bacon!* is an inventive story about a boy going shopping – and his struggle to remember the shopping list! As much of the story is conveyed by the pictures as the text.

### Introduction
Introduce the book *Don't Forget the Bacon!* by Pat Hutchins. Ask the children to predict the contents from the information on the front cover (the picture and the title). Read the story and discuss the illustrations. Explain the use of speech and thought bubbles. Then discuss how people remember things when they go shopping.

### Whole-class skills work
Model writing a list of the items in the story. Use the prepared food labels, or pictures of food items with the words written underneath, mounted on card, to help.

### Differentiated group activities
1*: Read *Don't Forget the Bacon!* with half the group, giving each child a copy of the text, if possible. Encourage the group to read the text with you, and pause while reading to allow the children to fill in some words themselves. Meanwhile the rest of the group should try, independently, to write their own shopping lists, using a combination of drawing and writing. Exchange tasks after about 10 minutes.
2: Write shopping lists using a selection of food labels, as in the Introduction.
3: Role-play in the class shop. Ask the children to buy the items listed on the prepared shopping lists.

### Conclusion
Select a few children to show the class their shopping lists and ask the others to try to read them. One child could take a shopping list and buy the items in the class shop.

### Introduction
Re-read *Don't Forget the Bacon!* and remind the children of the need for shopping lists. Model writing another list for items from the class shop, showing how a mixture of writing and drawings can be used. This should give all the children confidence to try writing lists.

### Whole-class skills work
Look carefully at the words that change in *Don't Forget the Bacon!* (farm eggs/fat legs/

clothes pegs). Ask the children if they notice anything special about the words 'eggs, legs and pegs' (they rhyme). Write the words that change, but rhyme, on the board or flip chart. Look for similar letter patterns (rimes) and which letters change (onsets).

### Differentiated group activities

1: Write shopping lists. The children can use a selection of food labels to help with the lists and then 'buy' the items in the class shop.

2*: Read *Don't Forget the Bacon!* with half the group, pausing for the children to read some words independently. Meanwhile the rest of the group should use plastic or magnetic letters to investigate the *-ake* rime using different onsets (cake, bake, hake, lake, rake, take, shake, snake, stake). Exchange tasks after about 10 minutes.

3: Write their own shopping lists, using a mixture of drawing and writing. Food labels and the teacher's sample list could be used as support.

### Conclusion

Group 3 children might share their shopping lists with the rest of the class. Finish by investigating the *-ake* rime with the whole class, using plastic or magnetic letters.

### Introduction

Discuss favourite foods with the class. Stick a selection of food labels on the board, or the wall, and pin or stick children's names next to their preferred food. Ask the children which foods are healthy and model making a simple poster about healthy foods. Include a heading and examples of healthy foods (these could be pictures cut from magazines or drawings).

### Whole-class skills work

Look for examples of capital letters – in the names of the children and on food packaging. Check that they know why we use capital letters (to show that the word is something important).

### Differentiated group activities

1: Make posters of healthy foods by sticking a selection of pictures onto A3 paper and writing a heading, using words that have been suggested and written up on the board or flip chart – possibly 'Healthy Food'.

2: Sort a selection of pictures into healthy and less healthy foods, using photocopiable page 126 (Healthy Foods – Or Not?).

3*: Make individual 'I like' books, drawing a picture on each page. The teacher should scribe a sentence for the children to trace or copy.

### Conclusion

Ask some of the children to show examples of 'I like' books and posters of healthy foods. Discuss which foods are healthy.

Look for further examples of capital letters in examples of food packaging, reinforcing the purpose of capital letters.

### Introduction

Write a variety of themed shopping lists to read with the whole class, perhaps items for a party, or items to make a sandwich. Ask selected children to demonstrate buying the products on the list in the class shop.

### Whole-class skills work

Play a game of 'I went to market and I bought' with the whole class, using items that begin with the same letter. The children have to remember, and repeat, all the items that have been said already and add a further item beginning with the same letter. Help some of the less able children by drawing a quick sketch of the items, as they are said, on the board or flip chart.

### Differentiated group activities

1: Sort a selection of food pictures into healthy and less healthy. The children should list the sorted foods under the headings 'Healthy' and 'Not healthy'. Photocopiable page 126 (Healthy Foods – Or Not?) might be useful for this.

2*: Make individual 'I like' books, drawing a picture on each page. Encourage the children to write a word underneath each drawing to complete the 'I like' sentence.

3*: Look through magazines to cut out pictures of healthy foods. Stick pictures onto A3 paper to produce healthy food posters.

### Conclusion

Ask some children to share examples of healthy food posters and 'I like' books with the class. Model writing a list of healthy food for the class to read, showing some matching pictures.

### Introduction

Talk about the children's favourite foods. On the basis that many will like chocolate, explain that you are going to match chocolate bar wrappers to the names of children in the class.

Make a chart by sticking or pinning children's name cards to the board or flip chart on which you have displayed a selection of chocolate wrappers. Then draw or stick arrows to link names to labels, showing who likes which bar. Model writing sentences using the framework: 'I like... but I don't like...'

### Whole-class skills work

Talk about the sound at the beginning of the word 'chocolate'. Write the word on the board or flip chart and explain that it is two letters together making one sound (a digraph). Ask the children to supply other examples of words beginning with *ch*. You could provide some objects to prompt ideas. Write the suggested words on the board or flip chart.

### Differentiated group activities

I: Write individual books entitled 'I like'. The children should draw a picture of something they like on each page and write a sentence which begins 'I like _____', adding 'but I don't like _____' with a further picture to illustrate something they do not like.

2: Cut out pictures of healthy foods and make these into posters. The children should write a title using words that have been suggested and collected on the board.

3: Sort pictures to find those that begin with the *ch* sound.

### Conclusion

A few children should show examples of individual books and posters. Finish by asking a few children to help you put *ch* items into a shopping basket.

# HEALTHY FOOD – OR NOT?

■ Cut out the pictures below and sort them into foods that are healthy and not healthy.

# Term 3

# EACH PEACH PEAR PLUM

## OBJECTIVES

| UNIT | SPELLING/VOCABULARY | GRAMMAR/PUNCTUATION | COMPREHENSION/COMPOSITION |
|---|---|---|---|
| READING FICTION AND POETRY<br>Stories with predictable structures and patterned language: *Each Peach Pear Plum* by Janet and Allan Ahlberg. | Develop 'book talk' vocabulary.<br>Distinguish words that represent characters' names.<br>Recognize key words.<br>Locate rhyming words in a text.<br>Generate words by analogy from rimes. | Understand that words are ordered from left to right and need to be read that way to make sense.<br>Use awareness of grammar to fit in suitable missing words.<br>Sequence sentences from the text. | Tell a story from pictures.<br>Identify nursery rhyme characters.<br>Match one spoken word to one written word.<br>Take part in shared writing of alternative versions of the text. |

## ORGANIZATION (5 HOURS)

| | INTRODUCTION | WHOLE-CLASS SKILLS WORK | DIFFERENTIATED GROUP ACTIVITIES | CONCLUSION |
|---|---|---|---|---|
| HOUR 1 | Shared reading of *Each Peach Pear Plum* using a Big Book.<br>Look at the cover to develop prediction skills. | Develop vocabulary that relates to books, such as: title, author, illustrator, character. | 1: Sequence pictures from nursery rhymes.<br>2*: Guided re-read of story and then re-tell from pictures, with half the group. Others listen to the story on tape (exchange).<br>3: Draw a picture based on a nursery rhyme. | Select pupils from each group to present their outcomes and elicit a response or discussion from the rest of the class. |
| HOUR 2 | Shared re-reading of story.<br>Emphasize rhyming words when reading. | Identify rhyming words by underlining with a non-permanent marker pen on acetate overlay. | 1*: Guided re-reading of story with half the group, identifying rhyming words. Others listen to the story on tape (exchange).<br>2 & 3: Match rhyming words (on card) to text. | Selected pupils from each group present their outcomes. |
| HOUR 3 | Shared re-reading of the story, looking for nursery rhyme characters.<br>Shared reading of related nursery rhymes. | Identify rhyming words in different nursery rhymes.<br>Demonstrate with plastic or magnetic letters how words can be changed using different onsets with rimes. | 1: Read nursery rhymes, identifying rhyming words.<br>2: Sequence pictures from nursery rhymes.<br>3*: Guided reading of nursery rhymes with half the group. Others listen to nursery rhymes on tape (exchange). | Selected pupils from each group read different rhymes and show correct sequences from nursery rhymes. |
| HOUR 4 | Shared reading of story, emphasizing one-to-one word matching. | Physical reconstruction of nursery rhymes.<br>Identify key words. | 1: Complete 'Jack and Jill' cloze exercise on photocopiable sheet.<br>2*: Guided reading of nursery rhymes with half the group. Others listen to nursery rhymes on tape (exchange).<br>3: Play key-word pelmanism. | Selected pupils from each group re-read nursery rhymes.<br>Identify selected key words.<br>Put key words from a nursery rhyme into a sentence. |
| HOUR 5 | Shared reading of story.<br>Shared writing of possible alternative versions of sentences from the story. | Look at alternative rhyming words to fit nursery rhymes. | 1*: Shared writing of alternative sentences.<br>2: Sequence jumbled sentences from the story.<br>3: Draw sequences for nursery rhymes in template provided. | Read alternative sentences.<br>Show examples of drawings for sequences of nursery rhymes.<br>Highlight alternative rhyming words. |

## RESOURCES

Big Book version of *Each Peach Pear Plum* by Janet and Allan Ahlberg (Oliver and Boyd, ISBN 005-004406-0) [optional] as well as a set of at least four small versions (Picture Puffins, ISBN 014-050919-4) and a taped reading of the story, a collection of nursery rhyme books which contain some of the characters that appear in *Each Peach Pear Plum* (and some of these rhymes on tape).

Writing materials, including: A4 paper, crayons, pencils, paper, adhesive, an acetate sheet (Big Book size) and non-permanent marker pen.

Photocopiable pages 132 and 133, plastic or magnetic letters, a cassette recorder, a magnifying glass, board or flip chart, pointer.

## PREPARATION

Enlarge and copy onto card one set of the sequencing nursery rhyme pictures from photocopiable page 132. These can be laminated for extended use. In addition photocopy enough of this sheet for Groups 1 and 2. Make enough copies of photocopiable page 133 ('Jack and Jill' cloze exercise) for Group 1.

Write each of the rhyming words from *Each Peach Pear Plum* onto a separate card (eg plum, Thumb, cupboard, Hubbard, hunting, Bunting, and so on). Make enough sets for members of Groups 2 and 3 to work in pairs. Make a list of the characters from nursery rhymes and traditional tales found in the text.

Type or write two lines of text from each page onto A4 sheets (different lines on each page). Write or type sets of selected high-frequency words onto card, sufficient for one group. Make one enlarged version of each page for groups 2 and 3 in Hour 2. Divide enough A4 pages into three equal boxes for Group 3 in Hour 5. Write or type out text from the book and cut this into separate sentences for Group 2 to reassemble in Hour 5.

## SYNOPSIS

A charming rhyming and repetitive text which plants characters from nursery rhymes and traditional tales within the context of an 'I Spy' game.

### Introduction and whole-class skills work

Display the cover of the Big Book. Ask one child to point to the words that tell the name of the book. What do we call the name of a book? (The title.) What do we call the person who wrote the book. (The author.) Ask if anyone can point to the words that tell who wrote this book. Point out that in this case there are actually two names. Tell the children that Janet Ahlberg is the person who drew the pictures (the illustrator) and her husband, Allan, is the author, the person who wrote the words.

Discuss what they think the book will be about. If they already know the book, ask if they can explain what is special about it. Look briefly at the illustrations so the children can get a 'flavour' of the book. Then read the book all the way through, pointing at the words to emphasize the direction of print.

Now re-read it, looking carefully at the pictures with the children. See how many details and characters they can spot. Do they know where all the characters come from?

### Differentiated group activities

1: Give each child a copy of photocopiable page 132 which contains three pictures of three different nursery rhymes, but with the events of the rhymes in the wrong order. Ask the children to cut up the pictures, arrange them in the correct sequence and then stick them onto paper (alternatively, provide the pictures already cut up and placed in an envelope). Supply a list of character names, so that the children can write 'I spy...' underneath each picture, with the name of the character filled in.

2*: Re-read the story with half the group, who follow the story in shared copies of the text. Ask them to look at the pictures and take turns to tell their own story from each picture. The remainder of the group should listen to the story on tape and identify as many characters as they can 'spy' in each picture. Exchange tasks after 10 minutes.

3: Ask the children to draw a picture based on a nursery rhyme they know. Make sure they understand that they should add sufficient detail to enable others to guess the characters so, for Miss Muffet, they would need to include a spider and a bowl. Provide a variety of nursery rhyme books for inspiration.

## Conclusion
Remind the children of how the text and pictures work together in this story. Then choose children from each of the groups to present the outcomes of their group work to the rest of the class. Find out how many characters the Group 2 children were able to spy in each picture and allow the class to guess which nursery rhyme the Group 3 pictures are of. Did the Group 1 children sequence the pictures correctly and which characters did they spy in them?

## Introduction
Re-read *Each Peach Pear Plum* using the Big Book. This time emphasize all the rhyming words by saying them loudly. Ask the class what was special about the words that you said loudly (they rhyme).

## Whole-class skills work
Place a sheet of acetate over the book and, using a non-permanent marker pen, underline the rhyming words on a page as you re-read. Ask a child to pick a rhyming word from a selection on card and then find the same word in the text. Do they notice anything about where the rhyming words are to be found on each page? (At the end of each line.)

## Differentiated group activities
1*: Re-read the story with half the group. Encourage the children to join in with the reading when they can. Ask them to look carefully at the pictures and to take turns to tell their own story from each picture. Encourage them to use the same vocabulary to tell their story as in the original and to say the rhyming words loudly. Meanwhile the rest of the group should listen to the story on tape, before looking carefully at the pictures in the book to identify as many characters as they can 'spy' in each picture and name them. Exchange tasks after about 10 minutes.

2 & 3: Give pairs of children the rhyming words from the text on card, and enlarged extracts from the text (remembering that only one copy of each extract can be made). Ask the children to match the words they have been given to those in the text, placing the word cards on to the extracts. Finally, ask the children to underline all the rhyming words in the extract, before drawing a picture to match the extract.

## Conclusion
Remind the children that they were looking for words that rhyme. Select a few members of each group to find rhyming words in the text and ask the Group 1 children which characters they were able to spy in the pictures.

## Introduction
Look again carefully at the cover of *Each Peach Pear Plum* with the children. Talk about all the objects they can see (plums, a bucket, a well, a cottage, a baby's dummy, sheep, a black cat, a bowl and spoon, and so on). Ask if they can think of any reason why those objects are there. (To represent the nursery rhymes and traditional stories referred to in the story.)

Read the back-cover blurb and ask about the significance of playing 'I spy' in the book. Who are they looking for? Read the story again but ask the children to look carefully in each illustration for a nursery rhyme character (tell them that they need to be detectives – some children could even be chosen to look with a magnifying glass). Show various nursery rhyme books and briefly ensure that they know what nursery rhymes are. Check that they can identify Mother Hubbard, Bo Peep, Jack and Jill in the pictures.

## Whole-class skills work
Read the related nursery rhymes and examine their rhyming words. Ask the children if they notice anything about the words 'Jill' and 'hill'. (They have the same letter pattern.) Use plastic or magnetic letters to demonstrate how to change the word 'Jill' into 'hill', then see if the children can think of any more words ending with the letters *ill*. Encourage them to notice that the initial letter needs to be changed to change the word.

### Differentiated group activities

1: Read assorted nursery rhyme books to identify rhyming words.
2: Sequence the nursery rhyme pictures from photocopiable page 132. The children should then write (or copy from the board) the name of each nursery rhyme.
3*: Guided reading of nursery rhymes with half the group while the rest listen to nursery rhymes on tape and try to follow in corresponding nursery rhyme books. Exchange tasks after about 10 minutes.

### Conclusion

Talk about the nursery rhymes mentioned in *Each Peach Pear Plum*. Select a few Group 1 children to read a nursery rhyme. Ask some children from Group 2 to show their sequenced nursery rhymes and let the rest of the class check if the sequences are correct. Finally, ask some children from Group 3 to identify a rhyming word and make the word with magnetic letters. Another child can then demonstrate how to make a different rhyming word by changing the initial letter.

### Introduction and whole-class skills work

Use the Big Book for a whole-class re-reading of the story, emphasizing how one spoken word matches one written word. Use a pointer to point to words as they are read and, later, choose a child to point. Highlight any words that are repeated (key words).

Then, using the prepared enlarged sequences of nursery rhymes on card (from photocopiable page 132), ask children to hold one card each and then line up in the right order. Once they have got themselves in place, recite the rhyme and ask the rest of the class to decide if the order is correct.

### Differentiated group activities

1: Complete the 'Jack and Jill' cloze exercise on photocopiable page 133.
2*: Guided reading of nursery rhymes with half of the group, ensuring that children are pointing to the words as they are read. The rest of the group follows nursery rhymes on tape and, if possible, recites them as well. Exchange tasks after about 10 minutes.
3: Use sets of key words on card to play a game of pelmanism.

### Conclusion

Select a few children to re-read nursery rhymes and ask some children from Group 3 to show some of their key words. Challenge them to put some of these words into a sentence. Finish by allowing the whole class to attempt the cloze exercise. This will reinforce use of context cues.

### Introduction

Re-read *Each Peach Pear Plum*, and then talk about writing alternative versions of the text. Demonstrate this on the board or flip chart: 'Tom Thumb eating rice, I spy three blind mice. Three blind mice on the floor, I spy Margery Daw'.

### Whole-class skills work

Using key rhyming words from the text on card as a prompt, ask the children to suggest further rhyming words and make a list of these on the board.

### Differentiated group activities

1*: Write shared sentences for alternative versions of *Each Peach Pear Plum*. Each member of the group should then choose one phrase and draw a picture for it. (Emphasize that they should try to hide the new figure each time.)
2*: Put jumbled sentences from the text (beginning 'I spy') back in the correct order.
3: Draw three separate incidents from a nursery rhyme on the prepared A4 sheets divided into three boxes. Copies of nursery rhyme books and sequencing cards can be provided to help with this.

### Conclusion

Choose some Group 1 children to read alternative versions of the text. and others from Group 2 to read out sentences which have been re-ordered. Group 3 should also show their drawings. Re-emphasize different rhyming words.

# NURSERY RHYME PICTURES

■ Cut out the pictures. Put them in the right order so they tell the story.

Jack and Jill

Little Bo Peep

Old Mother Hubbard

# JACK AND JILL

■ Fill in the words that fit in the nursery rhyme.

Jack and ____ll went up the h____

To fetch a pail of water.

Jack fell __own and broke his cr____

And Jill came tumbling after.

Up Jack got and home did trot

As fast as he could caper.

He went to __ed to mend his __ead

With vinegar and brown ____er.

■ Cut out the pictures and paste them next to the right lines.

| Jill | hill | down | crown | bed | head | paper |

# HUNT THE WORD

## OBJECTIVES

| UNIT | SPELLING/VOCABULARY | GRAMMAR/PUNCTUATION | COMPREHENSION/ COMPOSITION |
|---|---|---|---|
| READING NON-FICTION Simple non-fiction texts: Signs and labels. | Reinforce sight vocabulary of key words. | Find examples of capital letters and lower case letters. | Read signs and labels in the classroom. |

## ORGANIZATION (1 HOUR)

| | INTRODUCTION | WHOLE-CLASS SKILLS WORK | DIFFERENTIATED GROUP ACTIVITIES | CONCLUSION |
|---|---|---|---|---|
| HOUR 1 | Shared reading of notices and print in the classroom. | 'Hunt the word'. Identify key words on notices and print in the classroom. | 1*: Write sentences containing key words. 2: Track key words in a page of a newspaper. 3: Play a game of 'Pairs' or 'Snap' using key words on card. | Reinforce use of key words, by showing examples in the newspaper. Read examples of sentences which contain key words. Teacher writes a sentence for class to read. |

## RESOURCES

One large and two small sets of key words on card, enough extracts from a newspaper for each member of one group, highlighter pens, plastic or magnetic letters, board or flip chart, alphabet strip, teacher's sentence maker and individual sentence makers or word banks.

## PREPARATION

Choose examples of high frequency words from List 1 of the National Literacy Strategy. On card make one large set, and two small sets of words and laminate these for extended use. Ensure that there are plenty of examples of labels and signs around the classroom.

### Introduction and whole-class skills work

Tell the children that you are going to 'read around the room'. Point out examples of print in the classroom – labels and signs – and ask particular children to try to read them. Encourage everyone to participate in some way, if only with their own names (on cards or drawers).

Now, using examples of key words on card, such as 'the' or 'was', choose children to 'hunt the word'. Talk about the sentences found and read them aloud with all the class joining in. Write the words on the board or flip chart so that everyone can see them and point out examples of capital letters, possibly in the children's names. Then, using an alphabet strip, ask different children to match capital letters to lower case letters.

### Differentiated group activities

1*: Use individual sentence makers or word banks to make a sentence that contains the key words on the board. Read the sentence to the teacher, then write and illustrate it.
2: Track key words (one or two words which have been referred to previously, and have been written on the board) using a highlighter pen and a sheet of newspaper print. Children could count how many times the word 'the' is found.
3: Play 'Pairs' and/or 'Snap' with sets of key words.

### Conclusion

Ask the children in Group 2 to talk about how many times they found specific key words. On the board or flip chart write a few sentences which contain key words and ask the children to read them out.

Choose children to 'hunt the word' in the home corner – using key words on card. (Ensure that you provide a print-rich 'home corner' with a variety of types of print, including menus, recipes, lists, letters, telephone directories, magazines and so on.) Hand out sample plastic capital letters and ask the children to find a word with that capital letter.

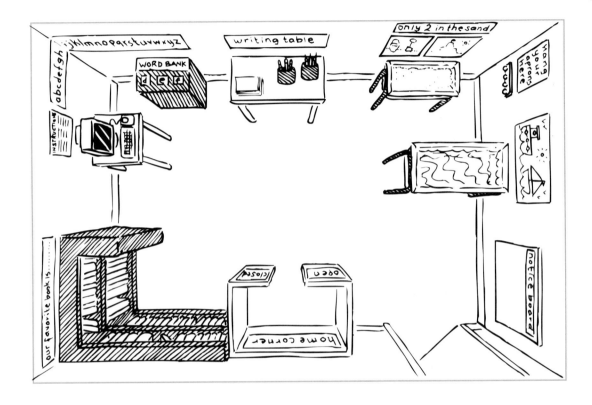

# MY DAY

## OBJECTIVES

| UNIT | SPELLING/VOCABULARY | GRAMMAR/PUNCTUATION | COMPREHENSION/ COMPOSITION |
|---|---|---|---|
| READING NON-FICTION Recount: *My Day* by B. Wade. | Read high frequency words on sight. | Match upper and lower case letters. Identify full stops. | Sort fiction and non-fiction books. Predict contents from covers. Understand the sequence of events in a recount. |

## ORGANIZATION (5 HOURS)

| | INTRODUCTION | WHOLE-CLASS SKILLS WORK | DIFFERENTIATED GROUP ACTIVITIES | CONCLUSION |
|---|---|---|---|---|
| **HOUR 1** | Shared reading of a Big Book non-fiction recount: *My Day* by B. Wade. Predict the contents of different books from covers. Discuss the differences between fiction and non-fiction books. | Match key words on card to the text and read surrounding sentences. | 1*: Guided reading of non-fiction recount with half the group. Others put sentences into correct order (exchange). 2: Sort books into fiction and non-fiction. 3: Play 'Pairs' game with key words. | Examine examples of books sorted into fiction and non-fiction. Sequence sentences from a non-fiction recount into the correct order with the whole class. |
| **HOUR 2** | Re-read non-fiction Big Book. Discuss the sequence of time, encouraging whole-class participation. | Use masking card to highlight key words. Individual pupils read surrounding sentences. | 1: Sort books into fiction and non-fiction. 2*: Guided reading of recount with half the group. Others match key words to sentences (exchange). 3: Draw the events to sequence 'My Day'. | Look at examples of pictures of different sequences of a day and write sentences to match for the whole class to read. |
| **HOUR 3** | Retell events from non-fiction Big Book with text masked. Add examples of text to match pictures. | Play 'Spot the letter' by choosing a capital or lower case letter on card and matching it to the text. How many examples can they find? | 1: Draw events to sequence 'My Day' and add sentences. 2: Alphabet cards – pictures for different letters, matching upper and lower case letters. 3*: Guided reading of non-fiction recount with half the group. Others match words to sentences (exchange). | Read examples of sentences from sequences of 'My Day'. |
| **HOUR 4** | Re-read the Big Book, making deliberate mistakes for the children to correct. | Read examples of sentences without pausing to show the need for full stops. Highlight full stops using acetate over the text. | 1*: Guided reading of a non-fiction book with half the group. Others match titles to books (exchange). 2: Draw events to sequence 'My Day' and label these. 3: Highlight examples of full stops on text. Put words into sentences. | Examine examples of labelling from 'My Day' sequences. Physical reconstruction of a sentence with the whole class. |
| **HOUR 5** | Read a fiction Big Book on a similar theme (eg *What's the Time, Mr Wolf?* by Colin Hawkins). Compare with the non-fiction book. | Scribe sentences for a typical day. Highlight use of key words. Whole class read sentences. | 1: Diary writing. 2*: Guided reading of book on theme with half the group. Others match words to titles (exchange). 3: Sequence pictures of 'My Day'. | Pupils read examples of writing from diaries. Whole-class matching of titles to books, identifying fiction and non-fiction. |

## RESOURCES
A non-fiction Big Book in the form of a recount, possibly *My Day* by B. Wade (Collins Pathways, Collins Educational, ISBN 0-00-30150-3), a fiction Big Book on a similar theme (*What's the Time, Mr Wolf?* by Colin Hawkins, Mammoth, ISBN 0-7497-1747-5) might be suitable), and a further selection of fiction and non-fiction books, one set of non-fiction recount texts for guided reading (these could be the same as the Big Book if available, but, in any case, are optional if you wish to use photocopiable page 140 instead), a further set of non-fiction recount texts for guided reading on a similar theme (see Hours 4 and 5).

Writing materials, including A3 paper, exercise books, pencils, Post-it notes, paper clips, sheets of acetate and non-permanent pens, spelling mats or lists of common words, board or flip chart, baskets for sorting fiction and non-fiction books, seal top plastic bags or envelopes.

Two sets of key words on card, a set of upper and lower case letters on card, picture alphabet cards, sentences from the non-fiction Big Book, masking card (see main Introduction, page 12), photocopiable pages 140 (My Day at School) and 141 (My Day).

## PREPARATION

Make two sets of key words from the non-fiction Big Book (from *My Day* these might be: day, school, book, teacher, like, mum, bed, home). Print out one copy of selected sentences from the book using large (48 point) font size. Laminate these, or paste them onto card, then cut them into individual sentences. Make picture alphabet cards by sticking pictures to represent letters on to card, then laminate these or cover them with sticky-backed plastic. Print or write the letters of the alphabet (both upper and lower case) onto card, laminate and cut into individual letters. Print or write a selection of titles of non-fiction books which you have in the classroom onto card.

Make enough copies of photocopiable page 140 (My Day at School) sequencing pictures) to have one for the whole class and enough copies of photocopiable page 141 (My Day) for one group. Divide one sheet of A3 paper per child into three sections and title these 'My Day'.

## INTRODUCTION

Introduce a non-fiction Big Book, such as *My Day*. Ask the children to predict from the cover what the book will be about. Read the blurb on the back and ask the children if they think it will be a story book.

Now read the book, talking about the pictures and pointing to the words as you read. As this is a recount it will need to be read in full. Ask the children if they found anything similar to their normal day. Talk about the information in the pictures and point out that these are photographs.

Now contrast this book with a fiction book. If possible, use a Big Book which has an illustration on the cover and which shows obvious differences. Talk about the differences between story books and information books. Use one or two further examples of story books and non-fiction books to emphasize the differences, showing the children the covers, and asking them to judge.

### Whole-class skills work
Using key words from the text on card, show the children one word at a time and ask different children to find the word in the text. Read the surrounding sentence with the class once the word has been located.

### Differentiated group activities
1*: Guided reading of photocopiable page 140 or a set of non-fiction recount texts (these can be the same as the Big Book if available) with half of the group, while the others work on putting sentences from the Big Book text into the correct order. Exchange tasks after about 10 minutes.
2: Sort a selection of fiction and non-fiction books into specially labelled baskets.
3: Play a game of 'Pairs' with two sets of the key words cards used in the whole-class session. Encourage the children to also match the words to the text in the Big Book.

### Conclusion

Examine examples of books which have been sorted into fiction and non-fiction to see if the class agree that they are sorted correctly. Sequence sentences from the non-fiction Big Book into the correct order with the whole class, referring to the Big Book to check that the order is correct.

**HOUR 2**

### Introduction

Begin by re-reading the non-fiction Big Book. Discuss the sequence of events with particular reference to times of the day. Talk about what the children in the class usually do at those times of the day.

### Whole-class skills work

Take a masking card with a sliding strip (see main Introduction, page 12) and, placing this over examples of the key words referred to in the previous lesson, read the words with the class, asking different children to slide the strip along and read the words which follow. Always read the whole sentence.

### Differentiated group activities

1: Sort a selection of books into fiction and non-fiction (as in Hour 1).
2*: Guided reading using photocopiable page 140 or a set of non-fiction recount texts with half the group. Meanwhile the rest of the group match key words to sentences from the text. Exchange tasks after about 10 minutes.
3: Give each child a sheet of A3 paper divided into three sections and titled 'My Day'. Ask them to draw pictures to sequence their own day.

### Conclusion

Select some Group 3 children to show their pictures and talk about the sequence of their day. Write examples of sentences to fit these sequences on the board or flip chart for the whole class to read.

**HOUR 3**

### Introduction

Take the non-fiction Big Book from previous lessons, and mask the text with Post-it notes. Retell the events from the pictures in the book, writing sentences to fit the pictures at the children's suggestion. Talk about the writing as you do it, for example: 'I am using a capital letter to begin the sentence. I must remember to put spaces in between the words.' and so on.

### Whole-class skills work

Play a game of 'Spot the letter' by choosing a particular letter on card (first ensuring that the children know which letter it is and can name it). Then find the chosen letter in the text, encouraging the children to count how many times they find the letter. Try this with upper and lower case examples of the same letter.

### Differentiated group activities

1: Give each child a sheet of A3 paper titled 'My Day', divided into three sections and with a line ruled about 8 cm from the bottom. Ask them to draw pictures to sequence their day and write a sentence underneath each section. Provide lists of key words to help with this.
2: Match upper and lower case letters to the alphabet picture cards. Matching pairs can be clipped together with paper clips.
3*: Guided reading of photocopiable page 140 (limit the number of paragraphs, if appropriate), or a set of non-fiction recount texts with half the group. Meanwhile the rest of the group match one or two key words from the text to sentences. Exchange tasks after about 10 minutes.

### Conclusion

Read examples of the sentences written by Group 1 children in their sequences of 'My Day'.

**HOUR 4**

### Introduction

Re-read the non-fiction Big Book, making deliberate mistakes when you come to key words. The children should put their hands up when they think you have read an incorrect word and tell you what the correct version is. You can differentiate this activity by varying the words you read wrongly (simple key words for the less able children to spot and more difficult words for the better readers).

### Whole-class skills work

Read selected sentences from the text without pausing at the full stops to emphasize the effect full stops have when you are reading. Place a sheet of acetate over the Big Book and ask the children to help highlight full stops by putting a ring around them.

### Differentiated group activities

1*: Guided reading of a non-fiction book, on a similar theme, with half the group. The rest of the group should match titles of non-fiction books (which you have written onto card) to the books. Exchange tasks after about 10 minutes.
2: Give each child a sheet of A3 paper titled 'My Day', divided into three sections and with a line ruled about 8 cm from the bottom. Ask them to draw pictures to sequence their day, adding words underneath each section, such as: morning, afternoon, evening. These can be copied from the board.
3: Placing a sheet of acetate over different books, the children highlight examples of full stops. They then take words from a sentence in the non-fiction text, and put them into a new sentence, ensuring they have the full stop at the end. (The words from each sentence can be stored in separate seal-top plastic bags or envelopes.)

### Conclusion

Ask a few children to show examples of the drawings that sequence their day and the labelling. Next, using words from one sentence in the text, choose the same number of children as words, give each child one word, and ask them to stand in the correct order to make a sentence. The rest of the class should read the sentence to see if it is right.

**HOUR 5**

### Introduction

Introduce a different Big Book, this time a fiction book. If possible, it should be on a similar theme to the non-fiction book already used so What's the Time, Mr Wolf? by Colin Hawkins would be a good choice. Ask the children to predict the contents of the book from the cover illustration, title and blurb.

Read the text, using a pointer to encourage the children to join in. When you have finished reading ask the class whether it was a story book or information book (you can also use the terms fiction and non-fiction). Discuss the differences between this book and the non-fiction book studied in the previous four hours.

### Whole-class skills work

Divide the board or flip chart into three sections and scribe sentences for a typical day for the class to read. Emphasize the use of key words.

### Differentiated group activities

1: Unaided diary writing about their day. You can provide a framework, such as:

     In the morning I ..............
     In the afternoon I ..............
     In the evening I ................

2*: Guided reading of a non-fiction book, on a similar theme, with half the group while the rest of the group match book titles to books (as Group1 in Hour 4). Exchange tasks after about 10 minutes.
3: Give each child a copy of photocopiable page 141 so they can cut out and sequence pictures of their day.

### Conclusion

Select a few children to read examples of writing from their diaries. Finish by asking the whole class to match book titles to the correct book, identifying whether they are fiction or non-fiction.

# MY DAY AT SCHOOL

My mum wakes me up at 7 o'clock.

I get washed and dressed and eat my breakfast.

I walk to school with my mum and my friend.

At school we sit on the carpet and my teacher does the register.

In the morning we write and take turns to read with the teacher.

We have assembly and then we go out to play. I like to play chasing games.

After playtime we do Maths. I like playing number games.

At dinner time I have a packed lunch and then I go outside to play again.

After dinner we sit on the carpet for the register and then our teacher explains what we are going to do in the afternoon. I like painting best.

We have an afternoon playtime and then it is story time. My favourite sort of story is one about children like me.

My mum collects me from school and we go shopping on the way home. If I am lucky we might buy some sweets or an ice-cream.

After tea, I read my school reading book with my mum.

Then its bath and bed time and ready for another day at school.

# MY DAY

■ Cut out the pictures and put them in the right order.

# OUR CLASS

## OBJECTIVES

| UNIT | SPELLING/VOCABULARY | GRAMMAR/PUNCTUATION | COMPREHENSION/ COMPOSITION |
|---|---|---|---|
| WRITING NON-FICTION Recounts: Our Class/All About Me. | Spell high frequency words, using visual features and spelling patterns. Link to handwriting practice. | Use capital letters appropriately, as for the start of names. | Through shared and guided writing, write simple recounts based on own experiences. |

## ORGANIZATION (5 HOURS)

| | INTRODUCTION | WHOLE-CLASS SKILLS WORK | DIFFERENTIATED GROUP ACTIVITIES | CONCLUSION |
|---|---|---|---|---|
| **HOUR 1** | Shared writing of introduction to book about the class. Use of photographs of class and individuals to stimulate writing. | Using one or two examples of high-frequency words encountered during shared writing, introduce pupils to 'Look-say-cover-write-check' routine for spelling. | 1*: Continue work on shared writing for class book. 2: Work on spelling books using words referred to earlier. 3: Play a reading game, using pupils' names. | Shared reading of 'Our Class' book so far. Selected pupils demonstrate the 'Look-say-cover-write-check' routine using words practised in spelling books. |
| **HOUR 2** | Re-read 'Our Class' book. Teacher scribes further sentences suggested by the class. | Spell high frequency words used during shared writing. Demonstrate correct letter formation. Pupils practise by 'sky writing'. | 1: Handwriting practice by making lists of pupils' names beginning with the same letter. 2*: Shared writing for 'Our Class' book. 3: Work with spelling books; practising words referred to earlier. | Shared reading from further extracts of 'Our Class' book. Sort pupils' names, on name cards, according to the first letter. Discuss sounds of first letter(s). |
| **HOUR 3** | Shared reading of 'Our Class' book. Add a contents sheet, with page numbers. | Choose words from 'Our Class' book to add to class word bank. Pupils put words in correct pockets. | 1: Spelling book work using high frequency words. 2: Handwriting practice of names. 3*: Guided writing of individual 'All About Me' books. | Selected pupils read from individual books. Examples of key words to be written for whole class to read. |
| **HOUR 4** | Shared reading of All About You by Catherine and Laurence Anholt. Selected pupils select items which could be used in their own 'All About Me' books. | Skim for specific words, such as 'hat' in the text. | 1: Make 'passports'. 2*: Guided writing of 'All About Me' books. 3: Draw a self-portrait, adding their name and age. | Show examples of passports, self-portraits, and 'All About Me' books. Complete a 'passport' form with the whole class. |
| **HOUR 5** | Re-read 'Our Class' book and All About You. Selected pupils choose items from the latter which could be used in their own 'All About Me' books. | Match words on card to text from All About You. Write a sentence made from words in the text for the class to read. | 1*: Guided writing of 'All About Me' books. 2: Make 'passports'. 3: Match words and pictures from the text. | Read an example of a passport and an 'All About Me' book. Match examples of words on card to the text. Skim the page as a class game. |

## RESOURCES

*All About You* by Catherine and Laurence Anholt (Mammoth, ISBN 0-7497-1297-X), dictionaries and picture dictionaries, individual A5-size books, spelling books, a blank Big Book, pages from newspapers or magazines.

Class word bank, children's name cards, high-frequency words on card, pictures and words from the children's 'All About Me' books, photographs of the class and/or individuals.

Writing materials, including yellow felt-tipped pen, Blu-Tack, board or flip chart, magnetic or plastic letters.

Photocopiable pages 147 (Passport Form) and 148–150 (All About Me).

## PREPARATION

Buy, or make, a blank Big Book (see main Introduction, page 10). Make an enlarged copy of *All About You* (see main Introduction, page 10) and prepare a set of words and pictures similar to those in *All About You* for different types of houses, toys, foods and places. This could be done by drawing or cutting out your own pictures, or by printing a selection using clip-art on the computer. Write a selection of key words from *All About You* onto card and make an additional set.

Make an individual 'All About Me' book for each child. This can be done by copying photocopiable pages 148–150, folding them and then stapling them together along the fold. Write on the cover 'All About Me, by ........' and then fill in details for each child, leaving a space on each page for a picture. (More able children may be able to write their own sentences inside the book.)

Make a copy of photocopiable page 147 (Passport Form) for each member of Groups 1 and 2.

## SYNOPSIS

*All About You* is a picture book which has a question on each double page spread with a group of different pictures for children to choose from, such as: 'When you wake up in the morning, how do you feel?' and 'When you look out of your window, what do you see?'. It provides a good stimulus for discussion of how we are all different, and for individual writing.

### Introduction

Explain to the children that you are going to make a class Big Book called 'Our Class' which will include information about all the children in the class. If possible use a class photograph and individual pictures of the children (taken either by a school photographer, or by yourself) to stimulate discussion. Begin by suggesting some sentences that might be included, such as:

This book is all about Class R.
We go to _____ Primary School.
There are _____ children in our class.
Here are the names of all the children:

As you write the sentences talk about how to spell some of the words and point out similar letter patterns. Talk about using capital letters and model spacing between words by placing a finger on the page before writing the next word. Ask the class to read back the sentences you have written.

### Whole-class skills work

Use one or two high-frequency words, perhaps 'is' and 'the', and explain that you are all going to try to hold a picture of the words in your heads. Show the children the words on card and fix them to the board with Blu-Tack. Ask one or two children to put the words into a sentence, ensuring that the sentences are meaningful.

Now talk about the shape of the word and the letters that are in it (in 'the', for example, you could point out that if you take the 't' away it makes 'he'). Draw round the shape of the words on the board and, when the children have taken a good look at each word, said it aloud, and written it in the sky with their fingers, ask them to close their eyes to see if they can still see the word in their heads. Remove the word from sight and ask one child to try to write it. Praise good attempts: 'Well done, you just missed out one letter'. Explain that the children need to do the same when they are working on spelling words individually.

### Differentiated group activities

1*: Continue shared writing for the 'Our Class' book with the children suggesting sentences for you to scribe.

2: Use individual spelling books to practise spelling high frequency words as in the whole-class skills work. The children can reinforce the correct spelling by making the words from plastic or magnetic letters and investigating further words using the same letters.

3: Play a reading game, using the class name cards. Take turns to pick up a card from a pile, try to read the name aloud and, if the name is read correctly, keep that card. When all the cards have been claimed, the child who has the most cards (or the most beginning with a given letter), wins.

### Conclusion

Let the whole class read the additional sentences written for the 'Our Class' book. Select a few children from Group 2 to 'be the teacher' and show the class a word on card for them to 'Look, say, cover, write (one child can do this, while the rest of the class) check'.

### Introduction

Begin by re-reading the 'Our Class' book. Then, using photographs of individuals, write a sentence at each child's suggestion: 'This is Gemma and she likes reading.' Do this for several children.

### Whole-class skills work

Practise learning the spelling of further high-frequency words using the 'look, say, cover, write, check' method. Emphasize the correct letter formation by saying: 'We write a letter a by going around, up, down and flick.' Children can practise writing the letter(s) using sky writing.

### Differentiated group activities

1: Provide name cards of all the children in the class for the group to sort into names beginning with the same letter. They should then practise their handwriting by making lists of names which begin with the same letter.

2*: Write additional sentences for the 'Our Class' book.

3: Practise spelling one high frequency word using spelling books. This group may need you to write the word several times, using a yellow felt pen, marking the correct starting place for each letter. They can then practise trying to write the word on their own. If you provide a page from a newspaper, or magazine, they can track the word and draw around its shape whenever they find it to aid their visualization of the letter pattern.

### Conclusion

Do some further shared reading of the 'Our Class' book. This can be followed by the class sitting in a circle and taking turns to sort the class name cards, looking specifically to see which names begin with the same letter. This should provide a good opportunity to talk about names which begin with the same letter, but do not begin with the same sound (Philip and Peter provide a good example).

### Introduction

Begin with a shared reading of the 'Our Class' book. Discuss the different pages and what is on each one, then explain that you are going to write a Contents page for the beginning of the book, which will show what is on each page. Number the pages and then write a title on each one. These will be listed on the Contents page, together with the page number. Ask one of the children to try this out by using the Contents page to find a certain child.

### Whole-class skills work

Scan through the 'Our Class' book with the class looking for any words which are not already included in the class word bank. Write any missing words onto card and ask a child to put them in the correct place in the word bank. (This can either be a commercially-made one with a large plastic pocket for each letter, or you could make your own – see main Introduction, page 11.)

### Differentiated group activities

1: Practise spelling high frequency words using the 'Look-say-cover-write-check' routine and spelling books. They might then try to find the word in a dictionary.

2: Handwriting practice of their own names, then, using the name cards, search for another child's name that begins with the same letter. Picture dictionaries might also be provided to find further words which begin with the same letter.

3*: Guided writing of individual books called 'All About Me'. The children should use the given format on photocopiable pages 148–150 to complete sentences about themselves. Some children may need you to scribe the missing words for them, using a yellow felt-tipped pen so that they can trace over your writing. Encourage them to draw suitable pictures in the boxes.

### Conclusion

Select some Group 3 children to show their 'All About Me' books and read out a few sentences. Show some examples of high frequency words for the whole class to read.

### Introduction

Show the children *All About You* (preferably using an enlarged version you have made). Ask the children to predict the contents from the cover and then read the book, taking time to ask different children to choose appropriate pictures of, for example, which kind of house they live in. Have some fun by deliberately making the wrong choices, such as a tent!

### Whole-class skills work

Now choose one or two words that are contained in *All About You*, perhaps 'hat' or 'house', and ask the children to move their eyes quickly across the page and put up their hands when they spot the selected words. They can then point to the word on the page. Read the sentence, if it is part of one. If it is a label for a picture, ask the children to check that it is the right word.

### Differentiated group activities

1: Fill out 'passport forms' using photocopiable page 147. This should include drawing a picture of themselves.

2*: Guided writing of 'All About Me' books using the format provided on photocopiable pages 148–150 (see Preparation, above). The children complete the sentences and draw a suitable picture to fit.

3: Draw self-portraits (mirrors can be provided) including as much detail as possible. They should then add their names and write their age.

### Conclusion

Show examples of self-portraits and passports and read one or two sentences from individual 'All About Me' books. Fill in a passport form, either for yourself or one of the children, with the whole class.

### Introduction

Re-read the 'Our Class' book and *All About You*, asking children to make appropriate choices from the latter that relate to their own experiences.

### Whole-class skills work

Using a selection of words on card from *All About You*, ask a number of children to match the words to the text. Then write a suitable sentence for the class to read, using specific words.

### Differentiated group activities

1*: Guided writing of 'All About Me' books. Any children who are able should add an additional sentence.

2: Complete 'passport forms' using photocopiable page 147. Write some of the words that will be needed on the board.

3: Use the words on card (used during the whole-class skills work) to match words to the text. Provide a further set of the words to allow the children to play a memory or pairs game.

### Conclusion

Read an example of a completed passport form and an 'All About Me' book. Choose a few children to match words on card to the text. You could make this into a race by challenging the children to see who can skim the page fastest. Ask them to put up their hands once they have found the words.

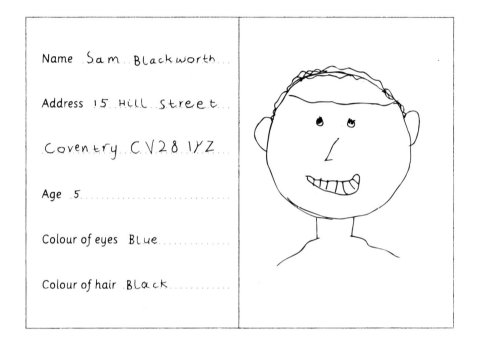

Name Sam Blackworth

Address 15 Hill Street

Coventry CV28 1YZ

Age 5

Colour of eyes Blue

Colour of hair Black

# PASSPORT FORM

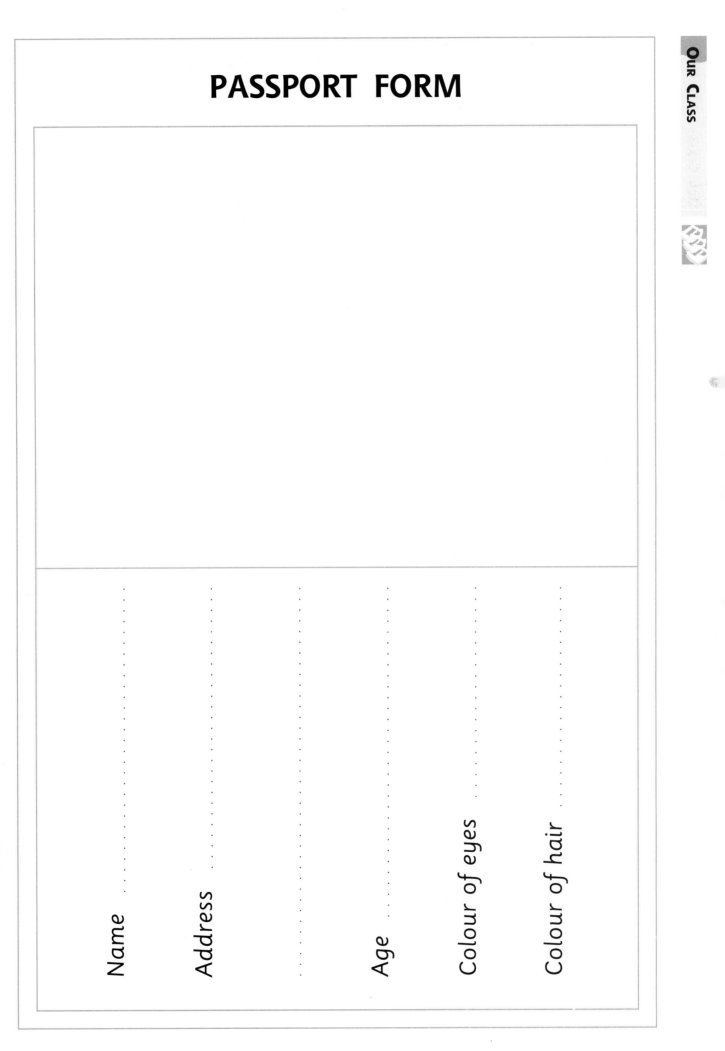

Name ........................................

Address ........................................
........................................

Age ........................................

Colour of eyes ........................................

Colour of hair ........................................

# ALL ABOUT ME: 1

lives with me.

I live in a

# ALL ABOUT ME: 2

I like to play with

I like to eat

# ALL ABOUT ME: 3

My favourite animal is

My favourite place is

# GOLDILOCKS AND THE THREE BEARS (1)

## OBJECTIVES

| UNIT | SPELLING/VOCABULARY | GRAMMAR/PUNCTUATION | COMPREHENSION/COMPOSITION |
|------|---------------------|---------------------|---------------------------|
| READING FICTION AND POETRY Stories with predictable structures and patterned language: 'Goldilocks and the Three Bears'. | Identify key words in the story. Match words with objects and pictures. | Use awareness of the grammar of a sentence to predict words. | Listen and retell a traditional story using story book language. Show an understanding of story structure. |

## ORGANIZATION (5 HOURS)

| | INTRODUCTION | WHOLE-CLASS SKILLS WORKS | DIFFERENTIATED GROUP ACTIVITIES | CONCLUSION |
|---|--------------|--------------------------|----------------------------------|------------|
| HOUR 1 | Tell the story of 'Goldilocks and the Three Bears' using props. | Using key words from the story written on card, read the words and match them to the correct objects or characters. | 1*: Guided reading of the story with half the group. Others listen to the story on tape (exchange). 2: Sequence pictures from the story in the correct order. 3: Play lotto, using words from the story. | Selected pupils show story sequences and examples of key words. Make key word sentences for the whole class to read. |
| HOUR 2 | Read a Big Book version of the story of Goldilocks. Discuss the structure of the story (actions and reactions). | Mask words in the text with Blu-Tack. Encourage the children to read on or read back to guess the word. | 1: Complete a cloze exercise from the story to develop contextual cueing. 2*: Guided reading of the story with half the group. Others listen to the story on tape (exchange). 3: Sequence up to four pictures in the correct order. | Selected pupils read examples of sentences from cloze exercises. Group 3 pupils hold up the sequencing pictures and talk about what is happening in different parts of the story. |
| HOUR 3 | Read different version(s) of the story. Discuss the differences and the common language used. | Model drawing a story map that shows the story sequence and includes some key words. | 1: Draw their own story maps, adding key words. 2: Put jumbled sentences from the story into order and illustrate. 3*: Guided reading of the story with half the group. Others listen to the story on tape (exchange). | Selected pupils display their maps, talking about what they show. Read examples of jumbled sentences. Ask different pupils to put them in the correct order. |
| HOUR 4 | Tell the story of Goldilocks using a wordless picture book. Emphasize the use of different voices and storybook language. | Write sentences from the story on the board, leaving gaps for pupils to fill in appropriate words (varying in difficulty). | 1*: Re-tell the story. Record own version on tape. 2: Role play of the story in the Three Bears' cottage using props. 3: Draw a story map. | Show examples of story maps. Pupils describe what they have drawn. Listen to a taped version of the story with the whole class. |
| HOUR 5 | Re-read the story from the Big Book. Re-enact the story with pupils taking different parts. Freeze-frame parts of the story to emphasize characters' expressions and feelings. | Highlight full stops in the text by ringing them on a sheet of acetate. | 1: Role play of the story in the Three Bears' cottage using props. 2: Draw a story map, adding some key words. 3*: Re-tell the story. Record own version on tape. | Selected pupils describe their story maps. Listen to taped version and discuss different versions. |

## RESOURCES

Various versions of the story of Goldilocks for comparison, including: a Big Book version (such as the one published by Kingscourt, Literacy Links), a wordless picture book version (such as the Collins Pathways version) and a guided reading set.

Photocopiable pages 155 (Goldilocks and the Three Bears Sequencing Pictures and Character Pictures) and 156 (Goldilocks and the Missing Words).

Props associated with story of Goldilocks – three different sized bowls and spoons, three chairs, three cushions (to represent beds!) and so on.

Lotto boards and sets of words from the story, key words from the story on card.

Writing materials including: A3-size paper for story maps, a masking device (Blu-Tack, or masking card), acetate, non-permanent pens.

A board or flip chart, a tape recorder and enough headphones and microphones for one group, a blank tape, puppets or a storyboard (optional), pointer.

## PREPARATION

Enlarge the pictures of the characters from photocopiable page 155 and make enough copies of the sequencing pictures for Groups 2 and 3 (this can be done in various ways – see Hour 1, Group 2, below). Photocopy enough cloze exercises (photocopiable page 156) for one group.

Make sufficient lotto boards for key words from the story for a group. These will need to be divided up into six sections with a word from the story on each section, ensuring that the boards are all different (photocopiable page 121 might be useful for this).

Make jumbled sentences from the story by writing out or printing some of the sentences and cutting them up into individual words. Write key words from the story (eg big, middle-sized, little, porridge, bowl, walk, woods, cottage) onto card. You might also put a relevant picture on the back of each card to help the children identify the word.

Convert the home corner into the Three Bears' Cottage, using the props you have collected. Masks would be helpful too.

### HOUR 1

### Introduction

Begin by telling the story of 'Goldilocks and the Three Bears' with real enthusiasm, emphasizing the different voices and using props to help bring the story to life. You could also use puppets for the characters or a storyboard.

### Whole-class skills work

Now talk about some of the words in the story and introduce the words you have written on card. If they have a picture on the reverse side this may help the children to guess what they say. Ask the children to match the words to the objects, or pictures of characters in the Big Book. You could also ask them to suggest sentences with the words put into a meaningful context.

### Differentiated group activities

1*: Read the story with half the group, using the guided reading set of copies of the text. According to the ability of the children, you may like to read this together. Meanwhile the rest of the group listen to the story on tape, following it in the text. (They could share an enlarged copy.) Exchange tasks after about 10 minutes.
2: Sequence pictures from the story (photocopiable page 155). This can be done by enlarging the pictures, colouring and laminating them, then asking the children to work together to put them in the right order, discussing the possibilities; alternatively, each child could have a copy to cut out and stick into the right order. The emphasis should always be on the discussion of the sequence, rather than colouring the pictures!
3: Play a game of lotto. Give each child a different base board (see Preparation, above). They then take turns to lift one from a pile of words on card to see if they can match with one on their board.

### Conclusion

Ask a few children to show their story sequences and explain the order. Show some examples of key words from the story and make sentences for the whole class to read. (You could use a teacher's sentence maker for this.)

## Introduction

Read the story of Goldilocks from the Big Book. Use a pointer as you read to emphasize one-to-one matching and the direction of print.

Now talk about the structure of the story. Explain that because something happens in a story then, as a result, something else happens (actions and reactions). Ask the children what happens to the three bears at the very beginning of the story and what happens because of it. ('The porridge is too hot, so the bears go for a walk and Goldilocks finds the cottage empty.') You might explore further actions and reactions in the story.

## Whole-class skills work

Now, using the Big Book of the story, mask different words with Blu-Tack or a masking card, and ask the children to guess the word. You could gradually reveal the first letter to give a phonic clue. Show the children how to read on to the end of the sentence or read back to the beginning to decide what the word might be.

## Differentiated group activities

1: Complete the cloze exercise on photocopiable page 156, using copies of the book to find the words missing from the story. Encourage the children to work together to find the words and talk about what they might be. When the cloze is completed the children should draw suitable illustrations in the boxes.

2*: Read the story with half the group, using copies of the text. The rest of the group listen to the story on tape, following the text. Exchange tasks after about 10 minutes.

3: Sequence pictures from the story (photocopiable page 155). For this group, limit the number of pictures to four.

## Conclusion

Select some children to read examples of sentences from the cloze exercises. Discuss whether they have made the right choice of words. Group 3 children should hold up the sequencing pictures and talk about what is happening in different parts of the story (the enlarged pictures could be used for this).

## Introduction

Begin by reading one, or more, different versions of the story. Talk about the differences and the similarities, pointing out, for example, the common language used and how the story begins each time.

## Whole-class skills work

Now model a story map (look back at the story map in 'The Gingerbread Man (1)' unit if you're not sure how to do this – see Term 1, page 57). Talk about the process as you do it and include as much detail as possible, encouraging the children to do the same.

## Differentiated group activities

1: Draw story maps, adding the names of characters and words such as 'woods' and 'cottage'.

2: Put together in the correct order jumbled sentences from the story (these can be cut up into separate words and put into different envelopes). The children can then write out one of the sentences and illustrate it.

3*: Read the story with half the group using copies of the text. The rest of the group listen to the story on tape, but also follow it in the text. Exchange tasks after about 10 minutes.

## Conclusion

Ask some Group 1 children to show their maps, describing what they have drawn. Read out a few examples of jumbled sentences and ask different children to put them in the correct order.

## Introduction and whole-class skills work

Tell the story of 'Goldilocks and the Three Bears' using a wordless picture book as stimulus (or other props or pictures associated with the story). Emphasize the use of different voices as you do this and appropriate storybook language. Now write, on the

board or flip chart, sentences from the story to fit with different pages from the book, but leave blanks for the children to choose words to fill the gaps. These could vary in difficulty to suit different abilities, but emphasize that it can help to read back or read on in order to guess the word.

### Differentiated group activities
1*: Retell the story using the wordless picture book (or other props). Emphasize again the use of storybook language and point out ways of making the story sound interesting, such as the use of descriptive vocabulary. Now record the group retelling the story. (If possible have individual headphones and microphones for this.)
2: Role play of the story of Goldilocks in the Three Bears' cottage. Explain to the children that they will all be re-enacting the story later.
3: Draw story maps, adding as much detail as possible.

### Conclusion
Ask some Group 3 children to show examples of their story maps and describe what they have drawn. Finish by allowing the whole class to listen to the Group 1 taped version of the story.

## HOUR 5

### Introduction
Re-read the story from the Big Book. Show the pictures of the characters from photocopiable page155, then re-enact the story, with Group 2 children taking different parts as they did in Hour 4. Freeze-frame parts of the story and ask the actors to show by their bodies and faces the characters' expressions and feelings. The rest of the class could help by suggesting suitable expressions and poses.

### Whole-class skills work
Now talk about how we can explain a story in text. Discuss the use of punctuation (full stops) to show us when to pause. Ask different children to highlight the full stops in the Big Book by putting rings around them (using acetate over the text).

### Differentiated group activities
1: Role play of the story of Goldilocks in the Three Bears' cottage.
2: Draw story maps, adding as much detail as possible and some key words.
3*: Retell the story using the wordless picture book, then record a group retelling of the story.

### Conclusion
Select some Group 2 children to describe their story maps. Let the whole class listen to the Group 3 taped version and then discuss different versions of the story.

# GOLDILOCKS AND THE THREE BEARS

## SEQUENCING PICTURES

## CHARACTER PICTURES

# GOLDILOCKS AND THE MISSING WORDS

Once upon a time there were _____ bears.
There was a _____ Bear, a
Mummy Bear and a Baby _____ .

They all lived together in a _____ in the woods.
One day, Daddy Bear made _____ for breakfast, but
it was too _____ .
They decided to go for a walk in the _____ while it
cooled down.

While they were gone, a little girl called _____ came
walking through the woods and saw the Three Bears' cottage.
She went inside and was so hungry that she tried to eat the

_____ .
Daddy Bear's and _____ Bear's porridge was too hot.
Baby Bear's porridge was just _____ , so she ate it up.
Next, Goldilocks sat on Baby Bear's chair and it_____ .
Goldilocks fell fast _____
on Baby Bear's bed.

The Three Bears came home and found Goldilocks.
She was so frightened she ran all the way_____ .

# GOLDILOCKS AND THE THREE BEARS (2)

## OBJECTIVES

| UNIT | SPELLING/VOCABULARY | GRAMMAR/PUNCTUATION | COMPREHENSION/COMPOSITION |
|---|---|---|---|
| WRITING FICTION AND POETRY<br>Shape books: based on 'Goldilocks and the Three Bears'. | Recognize common spelling patterns.<br>Collect words to describe characters.<br>Practise correct letter formation. | Use capital letters and full stops to denote a sentence. | Use experience of stories as a basis for shared and independent writing.<br>Write sentences to match pictures.<br>Draw pictures to denote the structure of a story.<br>Write letters using emergent writing. |

## ORGANIZATION (5 HOURS)

| | INTRODUCTION | WHOLE-CLASS SKILLS WORK | DIFFERENTIATED GROUP ACTIVITIES | CONCLUSION |
|---|---|---|---|---|
| HOUR 1 | Using story of Goldilocks, model drawing pictures to denote beginning, middle and end of story. | Use examples of CVC words, such as 'bed', to talk about the sounds and the letters used. Demonstrate 'Look-say-cover-write-check' routine. | 1*: Guided writing of pictures and sentences for beginning, middle and end of the story.<br>2: Draw pictures of characters in the story. Write their names.<br>3: Role play in 'Three Bears' Cottage'. | Selected pupils share examples of drawings to show the beginning, middle and end of the story.<br>Using the pictures of characters drawn by Group 2, write suitable sentences for the class to read. |
| HOUR 2 | Model drawing a part of the story. Write a sentence to fit dictated by the class. | Brainstorm words to describe characters in the story. | 1: Draw pictures of characters in the story. Add words to describe the characters.<br>2: Role play in 'Three Bears' Cottage'.<br>3*: Guided writing of pictures and sentences for the beginning, middle and end of the story. (Teacher acts as scribe.) | Selected Group 1 pupils share pictures of characters and words used.<br>Pictures of the beginning, middle and end of the story are also shown.<br>Act out Goldilocks in the 'hot seat', with the rest of the class asking questions. |
| HOUR 3 | Model individual books in the shape of the Three Bears' cottage with three pages to represent the three parts of the story. | Demonstrate correct letter formation with a group of lower case letters. | 1: Write letters from Goldilocks to the Three Bears with a given framework.<br>2* Guided writing of sentences for shape books.<br>3: Handwriting practice, of lower case letters. | Pupils show sentences from their books and letters to the Three Bears.<br>Sing 'When Goldilocks went to the House of the Bears'. |
| HOUR 4 | Model writing further sentences for individual shape books. | Collect examples of words from the story to put in class word bank. | 1*: Guided writing of sentences for individual shape books.<br>2: Handwriting practice using words from the story.<br>3: Write letters from Goldilocks. | Selected pupils show examples of shape books and letters from Goldilocks.<br>Shared writing of a letter from Goldilocks to the Three Bears. |
| HOUR 5 | Write a final sentence for the example shape book.<br>Read the class story of Goldilocks with the whole class. | Play 'lucky dip' where pupils choose one letter from a container and have to find the same letter around the room. | 1: Handwriting practice using words from the story.<br>2: Write letters from Goldilocks.<br>3*: Guided writing of sentences for individual shape books. | Pupils show examples of shape books and letters from Goldilocks.<br>Re-enact the story with pupils taking different parts and using different voices appropriately. |

## RESOURCES

A copy of *Okki-Tokki-Unga* (A & C Black, ISBN 0-7136-4078-2) – optional, but specifically the song 'When Goldilocks Went to the House of the Bears' – photocopiable page 161 (Letter-writing Frame).

Home corner arranged as the Three Bears' Cottage with assorted props (as in the previous unit).

Writing materials, including A3 and A5 paper, handwriting books, cottage shape books (see diagram below), board or flip chart.

A collection of lower case letters (plastic or wooden) in a container, sentence makers.

## PREPARATION

Divide A3 paper into three columns with a line ruled across the page about 5cm from the bottom. Rule a similar line across A5 paper. Make sufficient shape books for the whole class. Make enough copies of photocopiable page 161 (Letter-writing Frame) for the whole class.

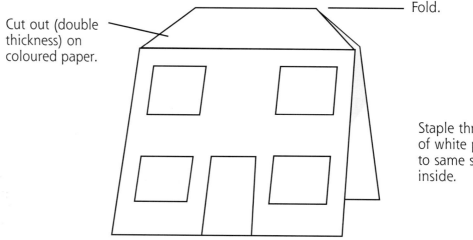

Cut out (double thickness) on coloured paper.

Fold.

Staple three sheets of white paper, cut to same shape, inside.

## HOUR 1

### Introduction

Remind the children of the story of Goldilocks. Explain that you are going to draw a picture of what happened at the beginning of the story. Talk as you do this, asking for suggestions of what should be included. When you have drawn the beginning, talk about the ending of the story, and ask the children to suggest what you should draw to show the ending. Finally, talk about what happened in between the two pictures you have completed (the middle) and draw a picture to represent this. This will help the children to talk about what happens in the 'middle'.

### Whole-class skills work

Using CVC words from the story ('bed' would be a good example), ask the children to talk about the sounds they can hear and which letters will be used to write them. Place particular emphasis on the final sounds in the words. Write up the words for the children to see and use the letter names when spelling them. Demonstrate the 'Look-say-cover-write-check' routine.

### Differentiated group activities

1*: Draw pictures to denote the beginning, middle and end of the story. Write sentences to fit each picture (with help).
2: Draw pictures of characters from the story on A5 paper, using a different sheet of paper for each character. They should then write the names of the characters underneath.
3: Role play in the 'Three Bears' Cottage' using various props.

### Conclusion

Ask a few children to share examples of drawings which show the beginning, middle and end of the story. Using pictures of characters drawn by Group 2 children, write sentences to fit each picture for the class to read.

### Introduction

Draw a part of the story for the class to describe, possibly Goldilocks looking through the window of the cottage. Ask the children to tell you when this happens in the story and ask them to suggest a sentence you could write to go underneath. As you write the sentence emphasize that you are using a capital letter for the beginning of the sentence, putting spaces between the words and a full stop at the end.

### Whole-class skills work

List the different characters and brainstorm words to describe them, both their appearance and their personalities. These words should be displayed for later group work.

### Differentiated group activities

1: Draw a picture of each character on A5 paper. Add words to describe them using the words collected in the brainstorm session.
2: Role play in the 'Three Bears' Cottage'.
3: Draw pictures to denote the beginning, middle, and end of the story. Write sentences to fit each picture, with the teacher acting as scribe.

### Conclusion

Select some children to share their pictures of characters in the story and words used to describe them. Show pictures of the beginning, middle and end of the story too. Finish by taking on the role of Goldilocks (in the 'hot seat') and allowing the class to ask questions about why she went into the cottage, ate Baby Bear's porridge, and so on.

### Introduction and whole-class skills work

Model writing in books in the shape of the Three Bears' Cottage, with three pages representing the three parts of the story. Write a sentence for the first page and discuss an appropriate drawing. Demonstrate correct letter formation, taking one or two letters from words commonly used in the story. The whole class can practise these using 'sky writing' and one or two children can also demonstrate on the board or flip chart.

### Differentiated group activities

1: Write letters from Goldilocks to the Three Bears saying sorry, using the frame provided on photocopiable page 161.
2*: Write sentences for individual shape books. One sentence should be written on each of the three pages to denote the beginning, middle and end of the story. Each one should have a suitable illustration. The sentences could be copied from the teacher's modelled sentence(s), or a sentence maker could be used.
3: Handwriting practice of letter formation of lower case letters in handwriting books. After practising individual letters – possibly *b, e, a, r* – they can try handwriting the whole word.

### Conclusion

Ask some children to show examples of their shape books and read some of their sentences. Some Group 1 letters from Goldilocks could also be read. If appropriate, finish the lesson by singing 'When Goldilocks Went to the House of the Bears'. Some of the key words from the song could be put onto cards to act as prompts, perhaps 'huge', 'small' and 'tiny'.

### Introduction

Read out the sentence that was written during the previous lesson as an example for the shape book. Ask the children for suggestions for a suitable sentence for the next part of the story (representing the middle) – hopefully previous work will enable them to do this. Write the sentence and ask the children to re-read it. You could talk about a suitable illustration to go with it.

### Whole-class skills work

Now, using examples of words from the story, write some words onto card for the children to see and read. You could talk about letter patterns and whether there are any other similar words they know. Ask the children to place the words into the class word bank. If you have a large wall bank with alphabetic pockets, different children could put the words into the correct pocket.

### Differentiated group activities

1*: Guided writing of sentences for individual shape books. Encourage the children to use previous work on the beginning, middle and end of the story to help.
2: Handwriting practice of letter formation of lower case letters in handwriting books or sheets, using words from the story.
3: Write letters from Goldilocks to the Three Bears using a mixture of emergent writing and drawing.

### Conclusion

Invite some children to show examples of shape books and letters from Goldilocks. Model writing a letter from Goldilocks to the Three Bears saying she is sorry. Involve the whole class in reading the letter.

**HOUR 5**

### Introduction

Finish writing the last sentence for the modelled shape book. Now read the whole book with the class.

### Whole-class skills work

Play a game of 'lucky dip' using a container of letters. Children pick a letter, one at a time, and then find an example of that letter around the room. They should also attempt to read the whole word.

### Differentiated group activities

1: Handwriting practice of letter formation of lower case letters in handwriting books or sheets, using words from the story.
2: Write letters from Goldilocks to the Three Bears using emergent writing.
3*: Write sentences for individual shape books. These can be dictated to the teacher to write, then copied underneath, or traced.

### Conclusion

Ask some children to read examples of shape books and letters from Goldilocks. Re-enact the story with different children taking parts and using different voices appropriately.

# LETTER-WRITING FRAME

Rose Cottage
The Woods

Dear Daddy Bear, Mummy Bear and Baby Bear,
I am very sorry . . . . . . . . . . . . . . . . . . . . . . . . . . . . . . . . . . . . .

. . . . . . . . . . . . . . . . . . . . . . . . . . . . . . . . . . . . . . . . . . . . . . . . . . .

. . . . . . . . . . . . . . . . . . . . . . . . . . . . . . . . . . . . . . . . . . . . . . . . . . .

. . . . . . . . . . . . . . . . . . . . . . . . . . . . . . . . . . . . . . . . . . . . . . . . . . .

. . . . . . . . . . . . . . . . . . . . . . . . . . . . . . . . . . . . . . . . . . . . . . . . . . .

. . . . . . . . . . . . . . . . . . . . . . . . . . . . . . . . . . . . . . . . . . . . . . . . . . .

. . . . . . . . . . . . . . . . . . . . . . . . . . . . . . . . . . . . . . . . . . . . . . . . . . .

Love from
Goldilocks

# ACTION RHYMES

## OBJECTIVES

| UNIT | SPELLING/VOCABULARY | GRAMMAR/PUNCTUATION | COMPREHENSION/ COMPOSITION |
|---|---|---|---|
| READING FICTION AND POETRY Action rhymes. | Explore rhyming patterns. | Know that words are ordered left to right and need to be read that way to make sense. | Re-read and recite stories and rhymes with predictable and repeated patterns. Make one-to-one correspondences between written and spoken words. |

## ORGANIZATION (1 HOUR)

| | INTRODUCTION | WHOLE-CLASS SKILLS WORK | DIFFERENTIATED GROUP ACTIVITIES | CONCLUSION |
|---|---|---|---|---|
| HOUR 1 | Say and sing a variety of rhymes with accompanying actions. Record the children singing on tape. | Use enlarged printed versions of rhymes and songs to follow the print, using one-to-one correspondence. Highlight rhyming words. | 1*: Re-read and re-tell the rhymes and songs. Oral cloze of rhyming words. 2: Choose a rhyme from the selection and draw appropriate pictures. 3: Listen to the rhymes on tape and join in. | Pupils show pictures and the rest of the class guess which rhyme it represents. Whole class reads rhymes and songs with the rhyming words covered so the children have to supply them. |

## RESOURCES

Photocopiable page 164–166 (Action Rhymes), writing materials including: A4 paper and Post-it notes, tape recorder, a blank tape, a published tape of action songs, preferably with accompanying text, a pointer.

## PREPARATION

Photocopy and enlarge the rhymes from photocopiable pages 164–166. (You may prefer to put each rhyme on a separate sheet.) Laminate them for extended use.

### Introduction
Introduce the rhymes: 'These are Grandmother's glasses', 'Where are you?', 'The Huntsman', 'Fox in a box' and 'Put your finger on your head' (all from photocopiable pages 164–166) to the children by singing or saying them and encouraging everyone to join in (many will already be familiar to them). When you have practised them a few times, explain that you are going to record their voices on the tape. Sing them again, this time recording it.

### Whole-class skills work
Now show the children the enlarged printed versions of the rhymes. Say them again, but this time use a pointer to point to the words as you say them. Talk about the rhyming words and explain that you are going to highlight the words that rhyme. Ask the children to help suggest which words you need to highlight.

### Differentiated group activities
1*: Sing or re-tell the rhymes with the group. Emphasize the rhyming words by saying or singing them louder. Now ask the children to listen while you say the rhymes, pausing at the rhyming words so the children have to fill in the correct rhyme. When you sing 'Fox in a box' explore rhyming patterns and then ask the children to suggest more examples of objects that rhyme with an animal for further verses, such as 'pig in a wig', 'bear on a chair', 'slug in a jug' and so on.

2: Choose a favourite rhyme from the selection that has been sung and draw a picture to fit that rhyme for the rest of the class to guess.

3: Listen to the taped version of the rhymes and try to join in. This could be followed by another tape of action songs, if possible with accompanying text.

## Conclusion

Selected children from Group 2 should show their pictures and the rest of the class guess which rhyme it is from. The whole class should then join in with the rhymes again, using the enlarged printed versions, but with the rhyming words covered with Post-it notes so the children have to supply them. Follow this up by writing the rhyming words on the Post-it notes to reinforce the one-to-one correspondence.

---

### The Huntsman

In a cottage in a wood.
(Make roof shapes with hands.)
A little old man at the window stood.
(Form a window with thumbs and forefingers.)
Saw a rabbit running by,
(Shade eyes with hand.)
Knocking at his door.
(Knock with fist.)

'Help me! Help me! Help!' he cried,
(Arms stretched out.)
'Before the huntsman shoots me dead!'
(Pretend to shoot.)
BANG!
'Come little rabbit, come with me,
(Beckon inwards.)
Happy we shall be.
(Make a petting motion.)

---

# ACTION RHYMES 1

## These are Grandmother's Glasses

These are Grandmother's glasses.
*(Make circles with thumbs and forefingers.)*
And this is Grandmother's hat.
*(Hands on head.)*
And this is the way she claps her hands
*(Clap hands.)*
And lays them in her lap.
*(Lay hands in lap.)*

These are Grandfather's glasses.
*(Make circles with thumbs and forefingers.)*
And this is Grandfather's hat.
*(Hands on head.)*
And this is the way he folds his arms
*(Arms folded, chin dropped on chest.)*
And has a little nap.
*(Snore gently or stay silent.)*

## The Huntsman

In a cottage in a wood.
*(Make roof shape with hands.)*
A little old man at the window stood.
*(Form a window with thumbs and forefingers.)*
Saw a rabbit running by,
*(Shade eyes with hand.)*
Knocking at his door.
*(Knock with fist.)*

'Help me! Help me! Help!' he cried,
*(Arms stretched out.)*
'Before the huntsman shoots me dead!'
*(Pretend to shoot.)*
BANG!
'Come little rabbit, come with me,
*(Beckon inwards.)*
Happy we shall be.'
*(Make a petting motion.)*

# ACTION RHYMES 2

## Where Are You?
*(To the tune of Frere Jacques.)*

*(Name of child in class)* Where are
you? Where are you?
*(Child replies)* Here I am, Here I am,
How do you do?
How do you do?

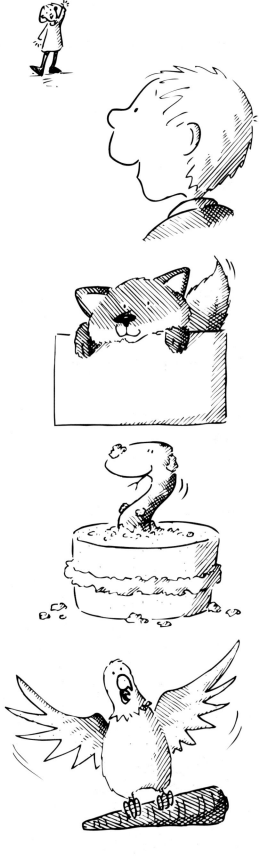

## Fox in a Box

There's a fox in a box in my little
bed, my little bed,
My little bed.
There's a fox in a box in my little bed
And there isn't much room for me.

There's a snake in a cake in my little
bed, my little bed,
My little bed.
There's a snake in a cake in my little
bed
And there isn't much room for me.

There's a parrot on a carrot in my
little bed, my little bed,
My little bed.
There's a parrot on a carrot in my
little bed
And there isn't much room for me.

*(Add further examples suggested by
the children.)*

# ACTION RHYMES 3

## Put your finger on your head

Put your finger on your head, on your head,
Put your finger on your head, on your head,
Put your finger on your head, tell me is it blue
or red?
Put your finger on your head, on your head.

Put your finger on your nose, on your nose,
Put your finger on your nose, on your nose,
Put your finger on your nose, tell me if the cold
wind blows?
Put your finger on your nose, on your nose.

Put your finger on your cheek, on your cheek,
Put your finger on your cheek, on your cheek,
Put your finger on your cheek, keep it there about
a week.
Put your finger on your cheek, on your cheek.

Put your finger on your ear, on your ear,
Put your finger on your ear, on your ear,
Put your finger on your ear, keep it there about
a year.
Put your finger on your ear, on your ear.

Put your finger on your finger, on your finger,
Put your finger on your finger, on your finger,
Put your finger on your finger, and your fingers on
your fingers.
Put your finger on your finger, on your finger.

# TOYS (1)

## OBJECTIVES

| UNIT | SPELLING/VOCABULARY | GRAMMAR/PUNCTUATION | COMPREHENSION/ COMPOSITION |
|---|---|---|---|
| READING NON-FICTION Simple non-fiction texts: *Toys* by Bobbie Neate. | Make a collection of topic-related words. Develop understanding of alphabetical order. | Use awareness of the grammar of a sentence to predict words when reading. | Understand and use correctly terms about books, such as cover, title, page and contents. Retrieve information from photographs and begin to devise appropriate questions. |

## ORGANIZATION (3 HOURS)

| | INTRODUCTION | WHOLE-CLASS SKILLS WORK | DIFFERENTIATED GROUP ACTIVITIES | CONCLUSION |
|---|---|---|---|---|
| HOUR 1 | Introduce the Big Book *Toys*. Predict and preview contents from cover, title, blurb and 'picture flick'. Read Contents list and select pages to look at. Examine and discuss photographs. | Make a list of types of toys from photographs in the book. Write words on card and fix them to the word wall of toy-related words. | 1*: Guided reading of non-fiction with half the group. Others, independent reading of a selection of books on toys (exchange). 2: Scan catalogues for types of toys. Stick pictures onto grids. 3: Using words from word wall, find same first letters as each word and match to alphabet strip. | Selected pupils show pictures of toys in categories. Pupils from Group 3 show letters matched to alphabet strips. Whole class match words from word wall to alphabet strip. |
| HOUR 2 | Examine photographs in the Big Book *Toys* and devise suitable questions. Write these onto card and fix them to the book with Blu-Tack. | Use an index from a non-fiction book. Choose words and match them to the alphabet strip. | 1: Scan catalogues for favourite type of toy. Cut out picture and write label. 2*: Guided reading of non-fiction with half the group. Others, independent reading of selection of books on toys (exchange). 3: Sort a collection of toys and match these to correct labels. Display. | Selected pupils from Group 1 show labelled pictures of favourite toys. Write a matching sentence for the whole class to read. Look at toys with matched labels. Read the labels to check that they are in the correct places. |
| HOUR 3 | Choose a further section of *Toys* to read using the Contents. Devise questions to match and think of suitable answers. | Add to class word wall of topic words. Talk about the first letter and match with the alphabet strip. | 1: Sort words from word wall into alphabetical order. 2: Label different types of toys. 3*: Guided reading of non-fiction with half the group. Others, independent reading of a selection of books on toys (exchange). | Look at examples of labelled toys. Devise appropriate questions to ask. Write these for the whole class to read and to answer. Sing an alphabet song or rap to reinforce alphabetical order. |

## RESOURCES

*Toys* by Bobbie Neate (from the Longman Book Project, ISBN 0-582-12277-5), a selection of non-fiction books on toys, catalogues containing pictures of toys, photocopiable page 170 (Toys Grid), writing materials, card, paper, Blu-Tack, glue sticks, scissors, plastic or magnetic letters, alphabet strips, a selection of different types of toys.

## PREPARATION

Prepare a word wall display area in the classroom, give it the title 'Toys', and mark it off

100 LITERACY HOURS ■ RECEPTION TERM 3                                                            167

in rectangles to make a brick wall pattern. Cut brick-sized pieces of card to fit.

Ensure you have alphabet strips in the classroom and, if not, make some. You will need one larger version for demonstration purposes and they should all show the upper and lower case letters next to each other.

Make enough copies of photocopiable page 170 (Toys Grid) for Group 2. Write the names of different types of popular toy onto cards which can be used as labels for sorting.

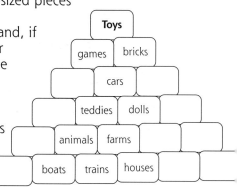

### SYNOPSIS

*Toys* by Bobbie Neate is a starter non-fiction book, which contains pictures of different types of toys divided into categories. The photographs are surrounded by large question marks to encourage the children to devise appropriate questions and find the answers in the photographs.

### Introduction

Begin by showing the children the *Toys* Big Book (or a similar Big Book on the theme of toys). If you do not have access to any suitable book you can make your own (see main Introduction, page 10, for instructions on making Big Books).

Ask the children to predict the contents from the picture on the cover, the title and the blurb on the back cover. Ensure that you use the correct terms: 'title', 'cover', 'author' and 'blurb'.

Now do a 'picture flick' of the contents of the book, explaining that a quick flick through the pictures will help us to know if the book is going to be about what we predicted.

Open the book and show the children the Contents list. Read the words, pointing to them at the same time, and encouraging the class to join in. Ask the class what they think the numbers might be for. Show the children that we can choose which part we want to look at, then find the part, looking for the appropriate page number. (You can start at the beginning and count the numbers on the pages to reinforce the use of page numbers.) When you have found the chosen section, show the children that the pages contain only photographs and no words. Some of them may be able to identify the question marks surrounding the photographs; if not, explain that these are to encourage us to ask questions about the pictures and look for the answers. At this stage, simply ask the children to comment on what they can see in the photographs.

### Whole-class skills work

Make a list of the types of toys found in the book. Write the words on card (which you have cut to the same size as the bricks in the word wall), ask the children to read them and then stick them onto the word wall.

### Differentiated group activities

1*: Guided reading of a set of non-fiction books matched to the group's reading ability with half the group. Encourage the children to use their awareness to predict words when reading. Use the same procedure as in the Introduction: predicting, flicking and looking at the Contents to choose a section to read or ask questions about. Meanwhile the rest of the group can be looking at a selection of non-fiction books on toys (or another theme), identifying photographs and what information can be gained from them. Exchange tasks after about 10 minutes.

2: Scan a selection of catalogues for pictures of appropriate toys to stick onto the grid on photocopiable page 170.

3: Working in pairs and using toy words from the word wall, find the same first letter from a selection of plastic or magnetic letters. Then match the letters to an alphabet strip.

### Conclusion

Select a few children to show pictures of toys on grids and read the labels. Some Group 3 children could give an example of a letter they matched to an alphabet strip. Finally, with the whole class, match some of the words from the word wall to a large alphabet strip.

### Introduction

Look again at *Toys*, select a further section from the Contents and ask the children to study the photographs carefully. Consider one photograph at a time and talk about it. Now ask the children for suggestions of questions to ask: 'Are these dolls old?'. They might also suggest answers they have worked out from information in the pictures. Write some of the questions on strips of card and fix them to the book with Blu-Tack.

### Whole-class skills work

Now use another non-fiction book, if possible on same topic, which contains a simple index. Choose words from the index, write these onto card and match them to the enlarged alphabet strip. These words can then be added to the word wall.

### Differentiated group activities

1: Scan catalogues to find favourite toys, cut out the pictures and stick them onto paper. If possible, they should label the toy with the appropriate word, using the word wall to help. Write 'My Favourite Toy' on the board, so that they can also copy this as a title.
2*: Guided reading of a set of non-fiction books matched to the group's reading ability with half the group. Encourage the children to use their awareness to predict words when reading. Encourage them to predict, flick and look at the contents to choose a section to read or ask questions from. Meanwhile the rest of the group should look at a selection of non-fiction books on toys (or another theme), identifying photographs and the information that can be gained from them. Exchange tasks after about 10 minutes.
3: Sort a collection of toys in the classroom and match these to the correct labels. This can form a display.

### Conclusion

A few Group 1 children should show their pictures of favourite toys. Write a matching sentence for each picture shown, which the whole class can read. Look at the toys sorted by Group 3. Ask the rest of the class to read the labels and see if they are in the correct places.

### Introduction

Choose a further section of *Toys* to read by looking at the Contents list. Select a section and ask a child to find the correct page number. Look carefully at the photographs and devise suitable questions to match, then write some of the questions on card to fix onto the book. Ask the children to think of suitable answers to the questions from the information in the photographs.

### Whole-class skills work

Use examples of words written when devising questions to write further names of toys to add to class word wall. In each case talk about the first letter and match it with the alphabet strip. Look through the book to see if there are any other toys that have not been included on the wall and add them.

### Differentiated group activities

1: Sort words from the word wall into alphabetical order using an alphabet strip.
2: Sort a selection of pictures of toys and write appropriate labels.
3*: Guided reading of a set of non-fiction books matched to the group's reading ability with half the group. (For this group the books will need to contain only a few words.) Predict, flick and look at the Contents to choose a section to read and ask questions from. The rest of the group should look at a selection of non-fiction books on toys (or another theme) to identify photographs and the information that can be gained from them. Exchange tasks after about 10 minutes.

### Conclusion

Look at the pictures of toys which have been sorted and labelled. Ask the class to devise appropriate questions, then write these for the whole class to read and to answer. Finish by singing an alphabet song or rap to reinforce alphabetical order.

# TOYS GRID

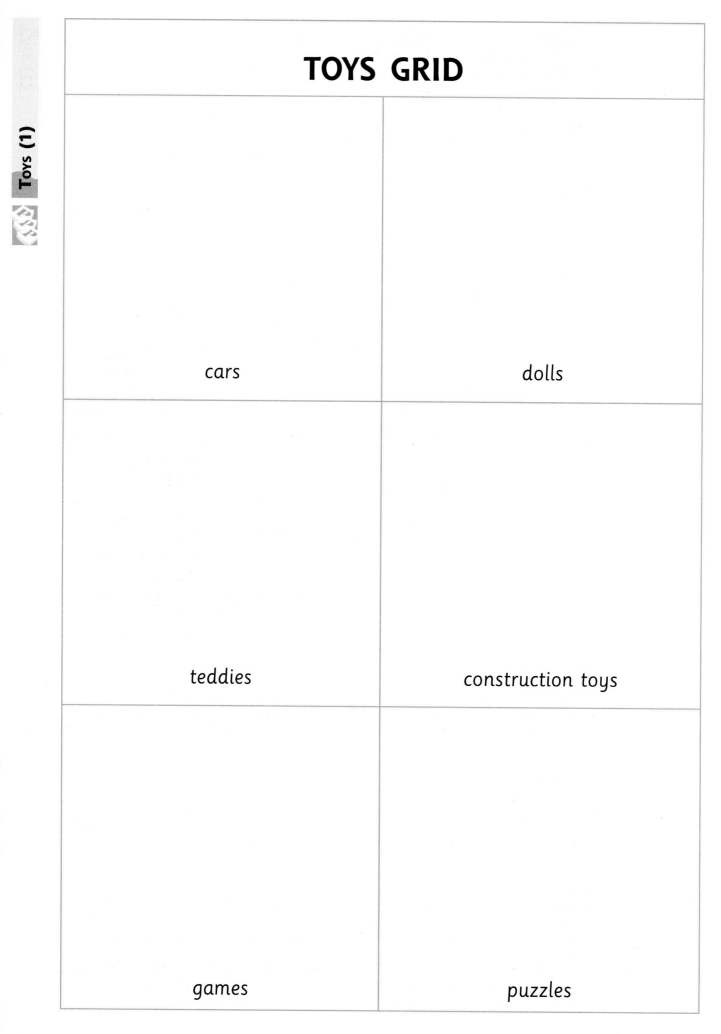

| | |
|---|---|
| cars | dolls |
| teddies | construction toys |
| games | puzzles |

# Toys (2)

## OBJECTIVES

| UNIT | SPELLING/VOCABULARY | GRAMMAR/PUNCTUATION | COMPREHENSION/ COMPOSITION |
|---|---|---|---|
| WRITING NON-FICTION Simple non-fiction texts: A toy alphabet. | Identify and write initial and dominant phonemes in spoken words. | Expect written text to make sense and check for sense if it does not. | Begin to make notes from non-fiction books by drawing pictures. |

## ORGANIZATION (2 HOURS)

| | INTRODUCTION | WHOLE-CLASS SKILLS WORK | DIFFERENTIATED GROUP ACTIVITIES | CONCLUSION |
|---|---|---|---|---|
| HOUR 1 | Read an enlarged book on toys with simple text. Model early note-making by drawing pictures to match the text. | Using a selection of toys in a bag, choose a toy and ask the children to help you write the word, talking about the different sounds and how they are written. | 1*: Guided writing of early note-making. 2: Make a toy alphabet, using a selection of pictures. 3: Match pictures of toys to the correct initial letter. | Show examples of note-making, with different children describing what their pictures show. Work with the whole class to think of examples of different toys to match a few letters of the alphabet. Write the words with pupils suggesting how they are spelled. |
| HOUR 2 | Show the children the pictures modelled in the previous hour and write sentences to match at their suggestion. | Continue with the toy alphabet using real toys or pictures and writing the words at the pupils' suggestion. Talk about choosing letters for each phoneme. | 1: Make a toy alphabet, using a selection of pictures and writing appropriate words. 2*: Guided writing of early note-making. 3: Sort pictures of toys into groups beginning with the same letter. | Show some examples of note-making and toy alphabets. Reinforce how letters are written in response to different phonemes by choosing various toys and writing the words. |

## RESOURCES

A Big Book on toys, such as *Toys* by Bobbie Neate (as used in the previous unit), photocopiable page 173 (Matching Letters to Toys), catalogues with pictures of toys, writing materials including A3 paper, board or flip chart, a selection of different types of toys in a box or bag.

## PREPARATION

Make enough copies of photocopiable page 173 for Group 3. Divide up A3 sheets of paper into separate sections for each letter of the alphabet, write on the upper and lower case letters, leaving space for a picture next to each letter.

### Introduction

Read an extract from the Big Book on toys. Make deliberate mistakes as you read and ask the children to spot what is wrong. Explain that we need to check that texts make sense. If you are using *Toys* by Bobbie Neate, read the questions and answers you devised in earlier lessons.

Model drawing pictures as a form of note-taking. On the board or flip chart make two columns with headings such as: 'Dolls we have now' and 'Dolls from a long time ago'. Draw some of the children's suggestions, but make sure first that the relevant pages in the book are not open and that the children can remember the details in the photographs. Explain that it is important to put plenty of detail into the pictures.

### Whole-class skills work

Using a bag or box with toys inside, pick a toy and ask the class to help you write the name. Talk about the sounds in the words and ask the children to say what sounds they can hear and which letters they would choose to write the sounds. Ask different children to select a toy, then try to write the word.

### Differentiated group activities

1*: Guided note-writing using a non-fiction book. Work as a group to choose a page, look carefully at the pictures, and read any words or captions. Help the children to write suitable headings so that they can then make detailed drawings of the information contained in the book.

2: Work as a group to begin constructing an alphabet of toys. Using the A3 sheets of paper already prepared with letters of the alphabet, children either stick pictures from catalogues or draw a toy to fit each letter. They may have to leave some blanks (it will be difficult to find an example for X).

3: Give each child a copy of photocopiable page 173 and ask them to match the pictures of toys to letters.

### Conclusion

Group 1 children show examples of their note-making, describing what their pictures show. Pupils from Group 2 show examples of toy alphabets. Now, working with the whole class, think of examples of different toys to match a few letters of the alphabet. Write the words, spelling them according to the children's suggestions.

### Introduction

Show the children the pictures modelled during the note-making session in the Introduction to Hour 1. Discuss what the pictures represent and write sentences to match that the children suggest.

### Whole-class skills work

Continue constructing a toy alphabet using real toys or pictures and writing the words that the children suggest. Talk about choosing letters for each phoneme: 'There are two phonemes in car – c and ar.' Ask the children to suggest the letters that should be used.

### Differentiated group activities

1: Work as a group to complete the toy alphabet using the A3 sheets from the previous lesson. Try to fill in any gaps.

2*: Guided note-making using a non-fiction book. Work as a group to choose a page, look carefully at the pictures, and read any words or captions. Help the children to write suitable headings so that they can then make detailed drawings of the information contained in the book.

3: Sort pictures of toys into groups beginning with the same letter.

### Conclusion

Select a few children to show examples of note-making and toy alphabets. Introduce the idea that one letter does not always make the same sound and reinforce this by writing down the names of different toys, asking individual children to suggest which letters form each phoneme.

# MATCHING LETTERS TO TOYS

■ Match the letters to the pictures.

# THE SLUG

## OBJECTIVES

| UNIT | SPELLING/VOCABULARY | GRAMMAR/PUNCTUATION | COMPREHENSION/ COMPOSITION |
|---|---|---|---|
| READING FICTION AND POETRY Poetry with predictable structures and patterned language: 'The Slug's Trail' by Wendy Jolliffe. | Discriminate onsets from rimes using the -ug rime. Notice the effects of alliteration. | Highlight the use of capital letters in poems. | Be able to re-read and recite rhymes with predictable and repeated patterns and experiment with rhyming patterns. |

## ORGANIZATION (1 HOUR)

| | INTRODUCTION | WHOLE-CLASS SKILLS WORK | DIFFERENTIATED GROUP ACTIVITIES | CONCLUSION |
|---|---|---|---|---|
| HOUR 1 | Read 'The Slug's Trail' to the children emphasizing the repeated lines. Encourage the children to join in, with one child chosen to point at the text. Discuss the slug's journey. | Highlight rhyming words. Use plastic or magnetic letters to make the word 'slug', then ask the children to make further words with the same rhyme. Investigate the pattern. Talk about words that begin with the same sound. | 1*: Guided reading of pattern and rhyme text, investigating onset and rime with half the group. Others re-read individual copies of 'The Slug's Trail' (exchange). 2: Investigate the -ug rime using plastic or magnetic letters. List the words made. 3: Draw map of slug's journey. | Select pupils from Group 2 to show the lists of words they have made that rhyme with 'slug'. Model a map of the slug's journey labelling it with rhyming words, such as 'rug', 'jug' or 'mug'. |

## RESOURCES

A set of any guided reading books which use pattern and rhyming text, photocopiable page 176 ('The Slug's Trail'), writing materials including A4 and A3 paper, non-permanent marker pens, plastic or magnetic letters, board or flip chart, a taped version of the poem (optional), audio tape listening centre and headphones, pointer.

## PREPARATION

Enlarge photocopiable page 176 onto A3 paper and laminate it to extend its use and enable easy highlighting. In addition, make sufficient copies of the poem for half of Group 1. Make a taped version of the poem (optional).

### Introduction
Begin by reading the poem 'The Slug's Trail' from the enlarged copy, using a pointer to point to the words as you read. Emphasize the rhythm of the poem as you read and the repeated lines. Ask the children what the slug was doing in the poem and see if they can identify the journey he made and that he returns the same way. Re-read the poem, choosing a child to point to the words as you read.

### Whole-class skills work
Ask the children if they noticed anything about the words in the poem (they rhyme). Then ask different children to highlight on the poem, with a non-permanent marker pen, the words that rhyme. You may like to re-read it as they do so.

Write 'slug' on the board or flip chart and use plastic or magnetic letters to make the word. Ask the children to tell you another word in the poem that rhymes with 'slug' and change the letters to make the word they suggest. Repeat this process for all the rhyming words in the poem, each time asking the children which letters stay the same and which change.

Re-read the poem, emphasizing the alliteration. Ask the children which sound they hear repeated (*s*). Then choose a child to point to the capital letters and put a ring around one or two. See if the children notice that a capital letter starts every line. If not, point this out.

### Differentiated group activities

1*: Guided reading with half the group, using a pattern and rhyme book matched to the children's reading ability. Investigate the rhyming words in the book. Give the rest of the group a copy each of 'The Slug's Trail' to re-read independently. Ask them to mark the rhyming words. Exchange tasks after about 10 minutes.

2: Investigate the *-ug* rime using plastic or magnetic letters. The children can work in pairs to make different words and then write a list of the words they have made.

3: Draw a map of the journey of the slug in the poem. (If you are able to provide a taped version for them to listen to this will help them to have a clear picture in their heads of the journey the slug makes.) The map should show clearly all the places the slug travels to. Encourage them to write a title, if they are able; if not, you could write this for them later.

### Conclusion

Ask children from Group 2 to read their lists of rhyming words. You could write these on the board so that everyone can see them and agree if they rhyme and share the same letter pattern. Now ask one or two children from Group 3 to show their maps of the slug's journey. If time allows, draw a map where the class can see it, labelling the objects that rhyme as you do so.

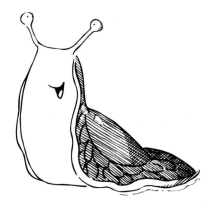

# THE SLUG'S TRAIL

Early one morning he started to slide
Across the garden freshly dug
Went the slimy slippery slug

In through the crack and into the house
Slowly trailing along the rug
Went the slimy slippery slug

Behind the cupboard and onto the jug
Silently climbing up and up
Went the slimy slippery slug

Then right on top of the best blue mug
Slithering smoothly round and round
Went the slimy slippery slug

Back he went where he had come
Down the mug and past the jug
Went the slimy slippery slug

Leaving his trail all over the rug
Into the garden freshly dug
Went the slimy slippery slug

*Wendy Jolliffe*

World's Best Gardener